Photobooks &

A critical companion to the contemporary medium

Matt Johnston
Edited by Emmanuelle Waeckerlé

ONOMATOPEE 220

4.
Photobooks & Access
Expanding a closed readership 101

5.
Photobooks & Reading
Establishing the role of the reader 129

6.
Photobooks & the Future
A reading economy and critical framework 159

To the makers, and the readers, as well as those who are not.

Yet.

Introduction

Despite a growing list of publications, conferences, workshops and curricula that take as their subject the contemporary photobook, there is a marked lack of criticality around the medium. Where a critical discourse is present, and where some more in-depth thinking has emerged, it primarily regards the photobook from the perspective of the maker, or considers it as a niche form of art to be treated with a certain reverence. By way of response, the role of the reader, the purpose of publishing and the contemporary situation of the photobook are some of the gaps in current conversations that I have sought to address in this publication.

↳ A response to restrictive discourse

The photobook in the post-millennium has stood against projections for an inevitable decline of interest in physical books, rebuffed the digital-only forecasts of some in photography, and provided a platform for numerous practitioners to share their works beyond the screen. But celebration of the medium masks a number of less encouraging attributes. In the late noughties, as I worked to engage undergraduate students with their university's photographic collection, I became increasingly aware of the hierarchical discourse that had mapped out a history of the photobook, and was proceeding to shape what constituted a good, or successful book. It appeared as though conversations around the role, context and relative merit of those photobooks included in recently formed canons had been cut short, and in their place was an emphasis on both the photobook as an art form, and on the very latest works emerging from around the world.[1]

To facilitate what I saw as missing conversations regarding the context of the photobook, I founded The Photobook Club in 2010.[2] It was begun as an online reading group intended to challenge assumptions of significance with regards to particular, canonised works — to open up discussion of the photobook in a non-hierarchical manner. Looking exclusively at publications published before the project's launch (and mostly works from the 20th century), personal reflections on photobooks from The Photobook Club community provided a voice for the collective, and global, reader to counter the role of the traditional expert and reject a dominant interest in the new.[3] The Photobook Club undertook 11 such readings, receiving many reflections each time from scholars, teachers, students, photographic hobbyists and historians.

In attempting to amplify and clarify the voice of the reader that had begun to emerge in these online

1
Though in the early days of the festivals, fairs, blogs and websites that came to construct the photobook ecology, there were far more works from North America and Europe than other portions of the globe.

2
www.photobookclub.org

3
It was a rare platform in this period in time, in that it was constructed almost entirely around both the reader and the historical (but not rare) photobook.

readings, as well as recognising the barrier that writing about an experience such as reading can be for many, I began to organise physical meetings. These operated much like a traditional book club, but rather than looking at one book, everyone attending was invited to bring a book and offer a brief introduction before it became part of the reading melée.[4] The philosophy of open discourse, and a non-assumptive and plain-speaking approach remained, ensuring that the event placed no emphasis on the education or experience of the individuals round the table, nor the accolades of books brought in. I ran a number of these events in Coventry and London before being invited to speak about the initiative at the London Design Festival. It was this platform that helped introduce The Photobook Club to communities in Barcelona and Madrid, after which, by word of mouth and the following of the project online, it grew to more than 50 locations in 24 countries by 2016.

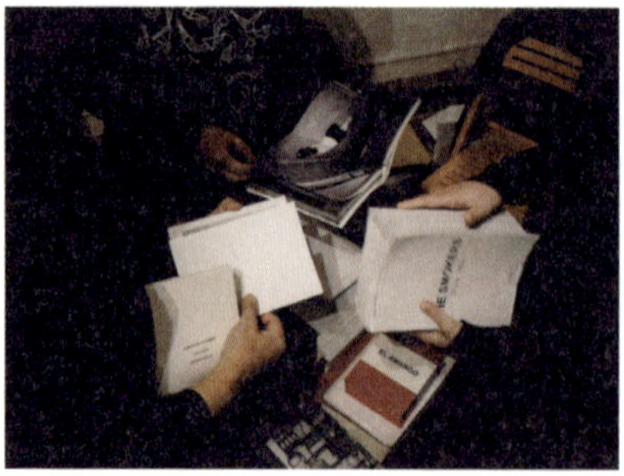

↳ A Photobook Club event in Barcelona, 2013. Image courtesy of Oscar Ciutat.

In each location, an organiser would take on the role I adopted when setting up the project — as facilitator rather than expert. They would organise the event, bring in additional books for those without and help to generate and synthesise discussion, but would not teach. This is something that Juan Cires of the prolific Photobook Club Madrid cites as being particularly important:

> 'The democratic aspect of the photobook club, the idea that we don't have the authority, we aren't teachers, we're not teaching people how to do things ... I think that's especially valuable and it's one of the things that I cherish the most when I think about The Photobook Club.'

Though each community has its own personality that reflects its participants and locale,[5] the ethos of openness, discussion and access is a binding principle.

4
Testament to the relaxed nature of The Photobook Club was the fact that coffee, beer and wine regularly featured among the books on the table. There has always been an understanding in the events I have run and attended that sharing a book without ceremony or concern is one of the great pleasures of owning it in the first place.

5
It was imperative for me in expanding The Photobook Club to encourage autonomy for organisers and the communities to which they belonged in a model of distributed authorship. I saw the franchise-like approach of projects such as TedX and Slideluck Potshow as replicating the hierarchical structure of the photobook ecology that I was trying to avoid.

These sessions, which to date have run into 1,000 hours of conversation, and The Photobook Club more broadly, however, are not without their limitations.[6] So while postal projects, pop-up exhibitions and the publishing of *Invisible City: A Digital Resource* (Johnston and Schles 2012) have contributed to patching some of the inadequacies I saw in a restrictive discourse, what remained was to see how my experience with the project could inform a more considered and holistic account of the contemporary photobook. By comprehending the circumstances of the medium in the post-millennium, how limited access to many books was, and the relationship between the makers[7] and their readers, I sought to introduce a critical companion to a predominantly celebratory rhetoric.

↳ Making, and making public

Working as part of the bookRoom research cluster with Emmanuelle Waeckerlé and with the support of Jean Wainwright and Camille Baker at the University for the Creative Arts, I developed the questions and lessons that had emerged from The Photobook Club into a more formal inquiry as a doctoral thesis titled *PHOTO / BOOK / CLUB: Connections Made and Missed, Digital and Other, Between the Contemporary Photobook and its Readers.* My aim with *PHOTO / BOOK / CLUB* was to provide a critical framework for understanding, debating and advancing the contemporary form of the photobook at a vibrant moment in the medium's life. In order to do so I set about examining the existing discourse and products associated with the photobook, as well as announcing and exploring a series of underrepresented aspects of scholarship regarding the purpose of publishing, its audience and the act of reading the photobook. Central to the argument I developed was the need for considerable thought regarding access, accessibility and readership — consideration not only of making, but of making public, too.

6 Including my own use of the word *club* at the outset: a term implying an exclusive group that may use particular language or operate in a manner that is difficult to penetrate.

7 I use the term *makers* to imply the team of creatives often responsible for the photobook in visual content, design and publishing of the work. Some books will have only one individual performing all these roles, but far more will have two, three or many more contributing to choices that lead to a photobook's launch.

It was evident on completion of *PHOTO/BOOK/CLUB*, that I should digest the findings of my work and reflect on how the existing form of my research as a thesis alone would fail to successfully reach and engage an audience of practitioners, librarians, students and critics with whom I wanted to speak. While it may be feasible to achieve this goal in extensive publicity and the construction of satellite events or outputs that revolve around the thesis, the content on which these acts must rely, and lead to, would remain a relatively dense and theoretical work. Instead, I intended to construct a comprehensive and practicable publication by revisiting, reworking and reimagining my research with a new purpose in mind. *Photobooks &* is the product of this process — rather than being poured into a new space, it has been rebuilt from its foundations.[8]

In this book, in addition to my own research on the photobook, I have strived to provide for readers a number of beginnings so that they may continue from where I leave off, or consider themes anew.[9] To accommodate different approaches to this book, the structure of the chapters means that they may be taken as a topic of merit on their own, or in linear form as part of the larger research project. Each chapter takes responsibility for a key connection between the photobook and the world beyond — starting with its situation in a post-digital landscape and as a focal point for a specific community before a consideration of intentions in publishing and issues of access. Then, I introduce a research-led account of photobook reading to forge a stronger bond between maker and reader, before turning my attention to the future of purposeful photographic publishing.

Throughout the book, the reader will be presented with thoughts and reflections from a number of individuals from within the photobook community. A large part of my methodology and a great influence on my findings, the conversations I have had with publishers, curators,

8
As an example, ten new interviews have been conducted to include the perspective of photobook libraries, archives and makers, which were less visible in the original research.

9
As well as a reference list, I provide notes that extend and depart from my research to conclude each chapter, a larger resource list at the culmination of the book, and offer a working definition of the photobook on the following pages.

It is proposed that what is presented here will continue and extend the core tenet of The Photobook Club in order to promote and enable a productive and critical photobook discourse. One that foregrounds purpose in publishing as well as a reading economy, and in doing so reconnects making, making public and critical discourse.

Photobooks &

photographers and scholars from the field are thus elevated on the page with the interviewees name underlined.[10] And, in addition to the words within these pages, a number of transcribed interviews that may help to progress our critical considerations of the contemporary photobook are available online at photobookclub.org/photobooks&.

↳ What is a photobook?

Returning now to the thinking behind The Photobook Club and its open discourse, I present a working definition of the photobook to be used throughout this publication. I often launched book club meetings with the question 'What is a photobook?'. It offered a way for the readers around the table to directly influence the books that would subsequently be brought in, and also led to passionate discussion. While here I cannot respond to the various voices of readers directly, the definition I construct is formed so as to include as many versions, or types of contemporary photobook as possible, without implying a hierarchy of worth or taste:

> The photobook is a single or multi-authored, bound work with photography as its primary content. It is an expression of a unified thought, subject, position, location or time, that has been constructed with awareness of the physical book as output.

This is a definition arrived at through analysis of extensive literature and the works appearing in festivals, competitions, exhibitions and my own bookshelf. I have stressed it as a working definition, and one that seeks to include rather than exclude, since I am very much in favour of challenges to the rigid confines of terminology whilst also finding it an essential point of reference to aid communication with the reader. This conflicted sentiment is echoed by Megan N. Liberty, who in her opening remarks in the Centre for Book

10
A complete list of the individuals I spoke to can be found in the interviews section.

Arts *Contemporary Artists' Book Conference* on criticism, used multiple terms to refer to the artist's book as a way to challenge institutional backgrounds and approaches to the field whilst acknowledging that such an approach 'muddies' the starting point for criticism. (Printed Matter 2021b). So the presence of the definition here acts as a beginning, rather than ending, for understanding the term *photobook*. But rather than simply presenting my working definition, it might be helpful to outline a few characteristics of other proposals I came across in my research.[11]

Most writing that has attempted to define the photobook places emphasis on productions that embrace a symbiosis of photography, sequence and design. They are holistic works. It is this convergence that formed a central part of one of the few early attempts to define the medium — by Alex Sweetman. Sweetman coined the term 'photobookwork' (1985, 187) as a way to stress the importance of the cohesive nature of a publication. The crux of the definition is in the disentanglement of books that feature photography in a random or purely aesthetic form, and those whose sequence relates to the conceptual aspects of the work. Sweetman defines the photobookwork as:

> 'A series of images — that is, a tightly knit, well-edited, organised group or set of images in a linear sequence presented in book form' (Sweetman 1985, 187).

This sentiment of cohesion is mirrored in John Gossage's statement featured in the introduction to Martin Parr and Gerry Badger's inaugural book on the photobook and its history:

> 'Firstly, it should contain great work. Secondly it should make that work function as a concise world within the book itself. Thirdly, it should have a design that complements what is being dealt with.

11
The definitions here evidence a separation from the field of the artist's book, which has its own discourse. While exploring the connection between the contemporary photobook and the artist's book is worthwhile, it is not the remit of this publication. As Sarah Bodman notes: 'You could say [photobooks are] within the field of artists' publications ... but I think it's really important that the distinction is there to make photobooks a bigger field rather than just saying it's a subsection.'

And finally, it should deal with content that sustains an ongoing interest' (Badger and Parr 2004, 7).

Other definitions place emphasis in different directions, or in relation to different themes of the photobook. Elizabeth Shannon, for example, highlights the book as 'an autonomous art form' where 'photographs lose their own photographic character, becoming parts of a dramatic event called a book' (Shannon 2010, 57), whereas Tate museum's definition looks at the pragmatics of publishing and makes prominent the low cost, and large audience for the book.[12] Alongside overt attempts to offer definitions, there are also competitions that, by their nature, must provide fairly clear guidelines on what is, and is not, considered a photobook, with examples from Aperture's Photobook Award[13] and the Kassel Fotobook Dummy Award[14] both accentuating the role of photography, and providing carte blanche over content.

It is evident that while there are crossovers in definitions, a lack of neat agreement makes trying to find a suitable place to lay a marker for the photobook somewhat difficult. This is one of the exciting things about our medium, and rather than quash or reduce it via micro-investigation, I hope that my proposal for a working definition provides some room for a malleable and moveable way of thinking about the photobook.

12
'The photobook is a book of photographs by a photographer that has an overarching theme or follows a storyline – a convenient and reasonably cheap way of disseminating the work of a photographer to a mass audience' (Tate n.d).

13
'A book in which the dominant content is photography, featuring the work of one or more photographer/artist, produced in physical form, and available for purchase or distributed free of charge, whether via trade distribution, print on demand, a gallery or online outlet, or otherwise' (Aperture 2021).

14
'Formally, a submitted work has to have the following criteria of a photobook: A photobook is a non-periodic collection of printed photographs (or reproduced on photographic paper) with text or even empty pages, with a binding and a cover. It can be made from paper or other suitable materials. There are no restrictions as to its content. It goes without saying that photographs are the major component of the book' (Fotobook Festival 2015).

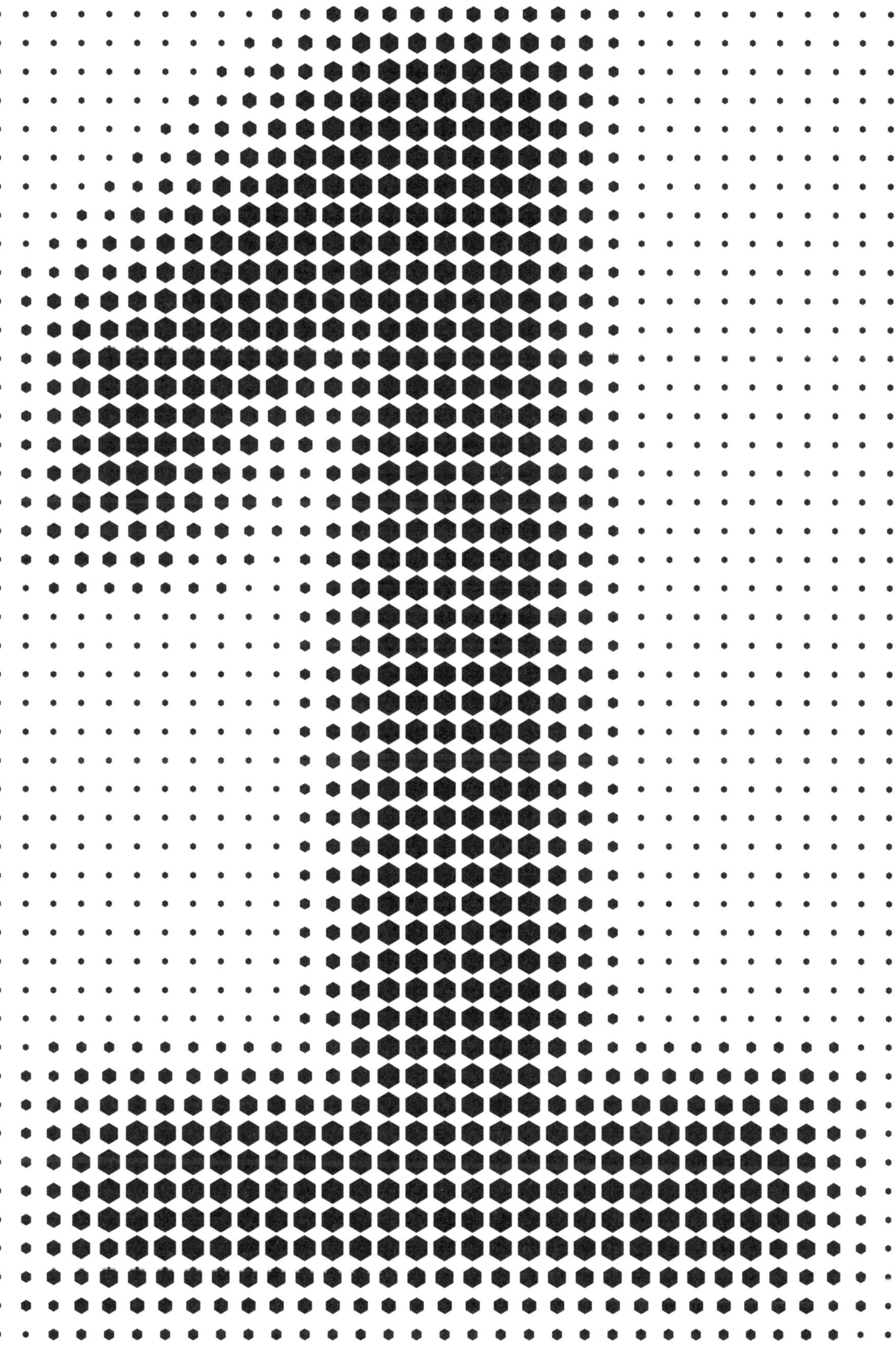

Photobooks & The post-digital

It is not possible to view the contemporary photobook and its new-found prominence in photography without acknowledging the part played by networked technology. The technisation of our professional and personal lives has provided the mechanisms through which to facilitate the prospering of the medium, and the background against which desires for such a tactile form of communication have been formed. The contemporary photobook exploits and soothes fissures that have been brought about in the rapid absorption of new technologies, and stands as a rebuttal to premature declarations regarding the death of the book.

Fig. 1

Naming the photobook; a range of terms encountered in research

Photographic book
Photographic artist's book
Photobook
Photo book
Photobookwork
Book of photographs
Photography book
Authored photography book
Photographically illustrated book

↳ The rise of the photobook

The photobook today is an inescapable 'phenomenon' (CCCB et al. 2017) in the photographic community, enjoying what could be described as a 'renaissance' (Rule 2015, 15), or 'golden age' (Tannenbaum 2012, 5). It is the subject of dedicated journals, blogs and websites, as well as occupying locations in niche bookshops, art galleries, museums and academy curricula. Whilst this elevated state has not been arrived at overnight, it is fair to say that it has been a relatively steep ascent. It is a position that has been announced not only in a plethora of accompanying activity,[15] but also in the unconscious agreement on the term *photobook* itself, which appears to have won out over the photobookwork (Sweetman 1985), photographic artist's book (Wilkie et al. 2012) and photo book (Crager 2014). The broad adoption of a dedicated term is not cause for all to celebrate though. It is an occurrence that frustrates some who, like David Campany, fear it homogenises a diverse selection of connected fields of practice: 'It's not an innocent word. It has been welcomed and taken up in order to impose some kind of unity where there simply was none and perhaps should be none' (2014).[16]

In addition to a conversation around nomenclature that has settled,[17] there are other indications of the significant growth of the photobook since the turn of the millennium. Books on photobooks, for example, have grown exponentially. David Solo charted the abundance of these publications in 2014 with a collection that included 50 titles, 44 of which were published after 2000 (ICP Library and Solo 2014). Then there are the many photobook-specific events and activities that have proliferated across the globe:

> 'As with any object-oriented, Internet-driven, niche culture at its best, this network has not been content to simply exchange information via blog

15
Such has been the boom of the photobook that many prominent photography magazines have gone beyond reviews and features to produce entire editions dedicated to the form: *YET magazine* in 2020, *Source* magazine in 2016, *The British Journal of Photography* in 2015, *Photofile* in the same year, *PDN* in 2013 and perhaps most significantly, Aperture launched the medium-dedicated *PhotoBook Review* in 2011.

16
Campany's fear is nothing new, with the same discussions taking place in the far more established realm of the artist's book for many decades — as seen in the mission statement for the College Book Arts Association *Art Theory Blog* (Minsky 2016) and in challenges to the classification of works that Michael Hampton explores in *Unshelfmarked* (2015).

17
Though differences in capitalisation remain — Photobook, PhotoBook, photoBook.

18 ↪
This data collection was first conducted for my thesis, which looked specifically at this area of the world. While in *Photobooks &* I have extended my research, the decaying nature of links and social spaces combined with retrospective searches make speaking with confidence about the history of dedicated photobook events in the rest of the world difficult. Rather than make assumptions on the completeness of events that I have been able to find, or presume that if events are not visible they did not happen, I have chosen here to retain only the US/EU data.

posts ... The in-person, hands-on experience has proven critical to the growth of the community and the appreciation of the objects being produced' ('Feting the Photobook' 2014).

In the US and Europe alone,[18] in 2015 there were 16 photobook-specific events (events with an exclusive focus on the photobook, see figure 2), 16 competitions, and ten dummy competitions, not to mention at least 31 bookmaking workshops. Particularly interesting to observe here is that of the 41 iterative activities (fairs, festivals and competitions), only one was running in any form in the 20th century (the Arles Book Award), and only four before 2010.[19] None of this is to suggest that photobooks were not being made, exhibited and recognised prior to 2010, but that the photobook was not regularly seen under its own steam (or name).[20] That is to say, more commonly the photobook would be included as an element within an exhibition on printed artistic works, a component of an artist's oeuvre, or as a historical reference point.

↳ Parallel emergences

Intensifying in tandem with a growth of interest in the photobook are networked technologies — technologies that no holistic or critical view of the medium should be able to ignore. Blogs to share photobooks, both owned and self-made, large discussion groups on Facebook, productions facilitated via Skype and Zoom conversations, digital offset and print-on-demand publishing, as well as specialist online retailers are just a few examples of the multiple ways in which the photobook has been enabled and impacted by our networked landscape.

In figure 3 we can witness two partial timelines together — the photobook, and networked technologies or their embodiments. This is not presented as direct causality,

19
A similar growth trend can be seen in the inaugural meetings of Photobook Club communities starting in 2011 with three, before a peak in 2013 with 17 new communities holding their first meetings.

20
This separation can be seen as a cause for celebration in the construction of a dedicated community, and a contributor to the richness of the contemporary medium, or as a worrying departure from key artistic, critical and political contexts, and is something at which I look more closely in 'Photobooks & intent'.

21 ↪
Jon Uriarte: 'We were all using Facebook at that time but it was also a moment of the blog. Everyone had their own blog so there were many things going on online and the conversation about photography and photobooks online was really happening at that point.'

22 ↪
Michael Mack speaking about the launch of MACK publishing: 'It was a fortuitous moment because it was 2010, when the first iPad was launched. That was the specific juncture and moment at which the notion arose that reading was going to change, that we were going to move to screens alone. Whilst that has happened to some extent, the reality is that that change has reinforced the possibilities of the analogue object. It's younger generations who appear to be cleaving more directly to the possibilities of ink on paper and the physical form of the book.'

European and North American photobook-specific events in 2015, together with their chronologies and continuations

*With the Covid-19 pandemic affecting events in 2020 onwards, the use of arrows indicate events planned, postponed or occurring in 2020 and 2021.

Fig. 2

Cosmos Arles Books	'15 '16 '17 '18 '19 ⟶
Feira do Livro de Fotografia de Lisbo	'10 '11 '12 '13 '14 '15 '16 '17 '18 '19 ⟶
Fiebre Photobook	'15 '16 '17 '18 '19 ⟶
Fotobok Festival	'09 '10 '11 '12 '13 '14 '15 '16 '17 '18 '19 ⟶
Fotobok Gbg	'15 '16 '17 '18
Kassel Festival	'08 '09 '10 '11 '12 '13 '14 '15 '16 '17 '18
Le PhotobookFest	'13 '14 '15
Photobook Bristol	'14 '15 '16
Photobook Market (Galleria San Rocco)	'15
Photobook Week	'14 '15 '16 '17 '18 '19 ⟶
Photobook Weekend (Photomonth)	'15
Polycopies	'14 '15 '16 '17 '18 '19 ⟶
Spine	'14 '15
Unseen Amsterdam Photobook Market	'12 '13 '14 '15 '16 '17 '18 '19 ⟶
Vienna Photobook Festival	'13 '14 '15 '16 '17
Athens Photobook fair	'15 '16 '17 '18 '19 ⟶

Fig. 3

A partial timeline of networked technologies alongside key photobook events and publications

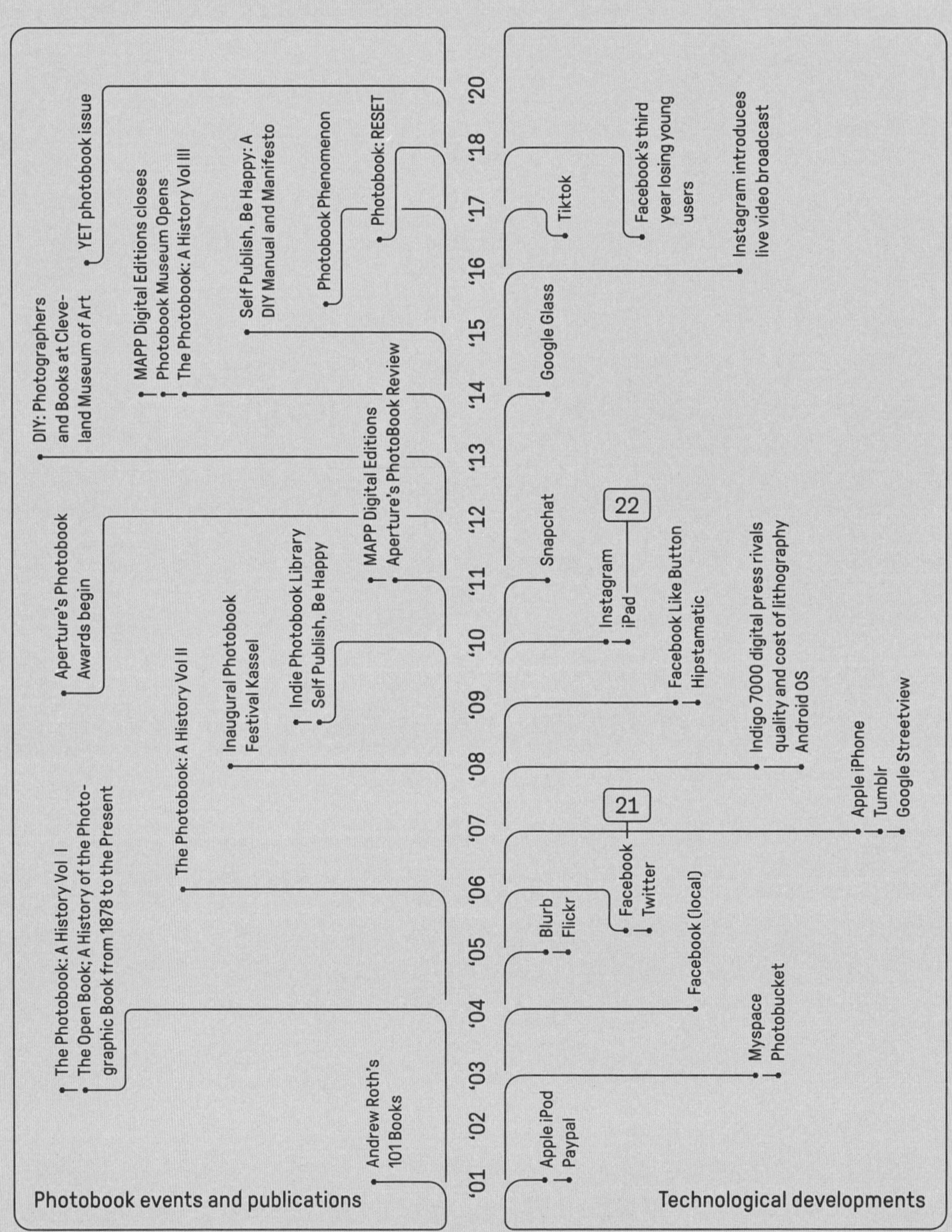

but connection. Identifying a correlation between an emergence of new technologies and platforms, and the rapid growth of photobook activity is useful in gaining a more complete understanding of the contemporary medium, but it only goes some way to explaining the photobook phenomenon: the myriad publications, events and other happenings witnessed so far. What an understanding of this correlation provides is part of the how,[23] but falls short of the why — for which we can turn to the post-digital.[24]

↳ A post-digital perspective

In the post-digital era we find ourselves surrounded, yet increasingly nonplussed, by technology.[25] 'Post-digital' is a term we can apply as much to works that try to reveal the messiness of our newly digitised lives as it is a way of speaking about the nature of the network as an 'undercurrent to our existence' (Openshaw 2015, 5). There are numerous and nuanced characteristics of the post-digital, which morph in relation to the fields and areas of studies to which they are applied, but some of the most relevant traits in a discussion of the contemporary photobook are found in hybridisation, disenchantment, grounding and code revelation.

Florian Cramer identifies the current use of old and new media alongside one another (2014), as well as the use of old media in a system that resembles new media formations as types of *hybridisation*. Kenneth Goldsmith provides an everyday example[26] in an observation of his students who 'mix oil paint while Photoshopping, and scour flea markets for vintage vinyl while listening to their iPods' (2011, 226). Sy Taffel in his writing on the post-digital extends the use of hybridisation to include 'a rejection of the binary oppositions of digital/analogue, human/nonhuman, nature/culture, and virtual/real' (Taffel 2015, 327). Thus hybridisation reinforces Cramer's notion that the post-digital

23
Taking a handful of publications on my own shelf and looking at this timeline, I am able to see a range of works that have been financed by crowdfunding, made using digital printing, sold or marketed through social networks and paid for by digital wallets.

24
The proposal here to consider the location of the photobook as inextricable from landscapes formed by digital technologies is not to ignore other influences on the photobook's growth. Certainly the publishing of Martin Parr and Gerry Badger's *The Photobook: A History series* (2005, 2006, 2014) (which followed on from Andrew Roth's *101 Books* in 2001) cannot be ignored, and nor can the complex forces that contribute to a lack of gallery spaces for emerging practitioners, or the decline of the traditional publishing industry that Bruno Ceschel cites. My perspective is that not only is a network-influenced perspective more often overlooked, but it also provides some of the most insightful reflections on our medium.

25
In thinking about the space of the photobook as primary within photography, as well as reflecting on the technologies and adoptions that bring about a post-digital culture, it is worth remembering that neither is absolute, uniform or evenly distributed. Instead, geographic, social, technological and artistic individualities are all contributors.

26
A number of other examples are presented in Karen Archey and Robin Peckham's introduction to *Art Post-internet* (2014).

‘should not be understood here in the same sense as postmodernism and post-histoire, but rather in the sense of post-punk (a continuation of punk culture in ways that are somehow still punk, yet also beyond punk)’ (Cramer 2014).

Where hybridisation is a unification of sorts between the analogue and digital, *disenchantment* speaks of a scepticism regarding the impact of networked technologies and a deeper questioning of linear progression from the old to the new (Berry and Dieter 2015, 4). It is a reaction presented in Cramer’s use of a ‘hipster-hating meme’ in which a young writer has taken his typewriter to the park. The choice seems at first a deliberate rejection of the digital, but the writer in question is producing short stories for passers-by, and with the aid of a typewriter is able to both write and print without power. Cramer posits this as an illustration of an individual who is ‘calling into question the common assumption that computers, as meta-machines, represent obvious technological progress’ (2014). Disenchantment, then, is not an adversary set of choices to counter the digital, but a move away from a presumption of merit in the higher quality, efficiency or speed that digital technologies tend to purport. There are, however, some choices in the post-digital that arise from a more conscious eschewing of the digital. *Grounding*, a term borrowed from Jonathan Openshaw (2015, 8), refers to the phenomenon of reaction to or protection against, the digital, where the value of the offline experience is heightened in its non-digitality.

Grounding is found in Kevin Kelly’s writing on embodiment as a valued generative that cannot be replicated by the internet or its associated machines (2008), and in Nathan Jurgenson’s coining of the ‘in real life fetish’ (2012). Jurgenson describes what he sees as a ‘backlash’ against networked technology and posits that an ‘obsession with the analog, the vintage, and the retro has everything to do with this fetishization of the

‘It started very much at the end of the noughties, 2010. I think there are a few reasons why it happened then. It was to do with technology … with the internet, which had become a powerful tool for distribution … and Facebook as well. There was also a general collapse of the traditional publishing industry towards the end of the noughties.’
(Bruno Ceschel)

‘[The] flowering of interest in the photo book has its roots in the rise of digital technology. The desire to own, touch, and hold visual arts in book form seems to have amplified in our increasingly virtual age.’ (Tannenbaum 2012, 5)

‘Whenever it seems that a newer, more powerful technology is about to change the established rules of a system, then that entire system tends to gradually produce a counter-reaction.’ (Ludovico 2012, 54)

offline' (2012).[27] Whilst this rejection is often overt, it is not absolute, since 'what is most crucial to our time spent logged on is what happened when logged off; it is the fuel that runs the engine of social media' (2014). Nor is grounding constant. We may well find objects and experiences that offer a certain tethering to the offline, but it is rare that this is not in conjunction with many other actions and engagements that are exclusively or partially produced and facilitated by the network.[28]

Last in our key themes of the post-digital is *code revelation*. This offers a way of speaking about the ways in which the workings of technologies are made visible. Code revelation refers to the glitch aesthetic and to works that 'reveal their own coded materiality'[29] (Paul 2015). For Hannes Bajohr, who borrows the term *technisation* from Hans Blumenburg:

> 'If the digital is a concept of reality or a temporality, increasingly transparent to scrutiny, the post-digital is what performs the sudden yank that makes it apparent again. It provokes a disharmony in the structure of the obvious, thus drawing attention to it, and makes the process of *technization* [sic] experienceable' (Bajohr 2016, 104).

I would adapt this description and the catchment of code revelation to also include those non-digital works that accentuate their own materiality or process and provenance. They too provide a 'sudden yank' of realisation, which is a reminder of the experience that the physical, haptic and non-digital can provide. In short, code revelation can, in this form, speak to a type of acute grounding.

The characteristics I have presented can be hard to disentangle, intertwined as they are with one another. We might illustrate this with a bookish example. The Espresso Book Machine is a printer[30] that, via a

27
'What I came to realise is that where our market was expanding most, for MACK, was in the really young students, who were supposedly digital natives. They're the ones — because their world is completely digital — who love the physical photobook, the physical art book, the art object' (Michael Mack in Jobey 2015).

28
Even remote and off-grid accommodation is likely to have been found and booked via digital services, with images or writings made in its confines shared later via networked technologies.

29
Works that draw attention to processes predominantly veiled from us by technology can be seen in many places: from the surge of glitch art, to hack labs that seek to unblackbox technology, and the introduction of musical genres like vaporwave, vaportrap and synthwave. The unblackboxing of technology can be attributed to Bruno Latour's construction of technology which 'blackboxes' — in that its 'technical work is made invisible by its own success' and that 'the more science and technology succeed, the more opaque and obscure they become' (1999, 304).

30
One could easily argue that it is also a bookbinder, shop and catalogue all in one.

networked connection to thousands of written works, and the speed of digital printing, is able to produce for a user a physical book to their own specification in minutes (On Demand Books 2016). The machine demonstrates not only a hybrid approach to production (new technology— internet of things, old technology — the book) but also the thought and choice of the reader or consumer — a move away from technological fascination. The Espresso Book Machine makes very apparent the bringing into a corporeal world a text that is readily available in a fluid, digital state and with it, a post-digital choice.

We are often able to witness the impact and manifestation of post-digital themes in the everyday: from the design of contemporary cafés and bars with exposed lighting and (implied) industrial furniture, to contemporary performances of materiality on cookery shows and even an increasing popularity of wilderness or escape vlogs on YouTube. The impact can also be seen on the contemporary photobook. The mere act of printing photographs is itself a rebuttal of the linearity of progression through digital technology, and demonstrates not only disenchantment, but a hybridised approach too — for few photographs contained within photobooks have not been made on, translated through or found with, digital hardware and software.[31] Then there is the desire of the maker and reader alike to engage with the tactile form of the book, which is a comparatively expensive and materially demanding object that provides a grounding for its participants in a real-world experience.

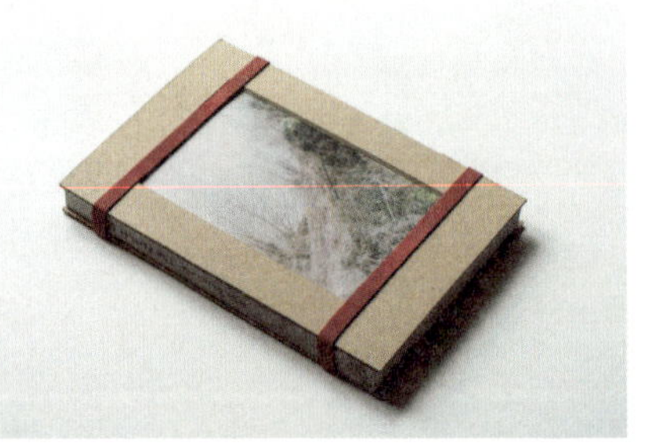

⌞ Julia Borissova's *The Father Shore* (2013), an example of the photobook's new materiality. Image courtesy of the artist.

Code revelation, and an interest in accentuating and presenting process is also common in the contemporary iteration of the photobook. I suggest that the desire to expose and display the workings of the photobook itself is in response to increasingly veiled digital technology. It may partly be why so many naked-bound

31
The catalogue of Jean Boîte Editions and The Library of the Printed Web are interesting projects to look at in relation to hybridised publishing. The photobook also exhibits hybridisation in the circulation of old media (the book), through new media in the form of various social-media sites, blogs and so on.

books have emerged alongside textured-cloth covers and muted tones:[32] these works reveal a construction that acts as a banner for corporeal existence. An even more prominent illustration of the photobook's situation in relation to the post-digital and an emphasis on production and process can be found in the increased visibility of the photobook dummy. The dummy book[33] is itself not a new object along the journey of publication, but in the post-digital, it has moved from the relatively private to the frequently public, with dummy-specific competitions and fairs proliferating since the late noughties. The dummy offers a view to the workings of the photobook[34] and a space of experimentation without considerable risk for the maker.

Collectively, what is witnessed here shows how the photobook's physical and haptic qualities are central to its prosperity in the post-millennium. When Florian Cramer speaks of contemporary zines and super-8 films, he suggests that they 'focus less on content and more on pure materiality', and I would position the photobook, having undergone a 'shift from semantics to pragmatics, and from metaphysics to ontology' (Cramer 2014), in the same manner. Already we are witnessing resonances between the post-digital and the contemporary photobook, but the situation of the medium can be made clearer still by looking at how it provides for photographers a means of reply to enormous technological shifts that have occurred since the early 1990s.

↳ A post-photographic perspective

Inevitably, changes brought about with the introduction of networked technologies have had a dramatic effect on photography in its many guises, and post-photographic discourse concerns itself with these adjustments. Not only does it focus on how digitised processes and the convergence of technologies have shaped the last three decades of technological

32
In addition to the pullouts, textured papers, replications of letters or documents and other ephemera that have been a feature of many highly awarded photobooks in the post-millennium.

33
The dummy is a proof version of a book that has historically been used as a step towards publishing an edition and is sent to prospective publishers, shown to friends and colleagues for feedback, or used to aid conversations with printers regarding production.

34
Interest in the dummy is also an indicator of an audience comprised of other makers — something that is a focus of 'Photobooks & community'.

development, but in turn on how this has led to a point where the photograph is now a type of 'algorithmic image' (Rubenstein and Sluis 2013, 29). The post-photographic[35] is a framework that seeks to comprehend the radical recalibrations of what was once understood about the construction, reception and behaviour of the photographic image and how it has morphed, or been entirely re-drawn. As with the post-digital, central characteristics of the post-photographic (in image abundance, fluidity and a questioning of veracity) are outlined here, and while not exhaustive, provide an introduction for those unfamiliar with the term.

Firstly, due to the proliferation of cheap and to-hand cameras (often embedded within phones), as well as a rapid decrease in the cost of digital storage, the sheer quantity of images produced by professional and amateur alike has multiplied. This abundance of imagery has caused many to bemoan a flood of images that could engulf photography. Erik Kessels visualised and concretised the metaphor in an installation of printed images from 24 hours of Flickr uploads, which were piled up on the FOAM gallery floors in Amsterdam (Kessels 2011). Only a year later, James Estrin of the *New York Times* spoke about the innocence of the professional photographers at Perpignan festival, in the face of the 'tsunami of vernacular photographs about to wash away everything in its path' (Estrin 2012). This profusion of digital images is made possible in part by the transformation of the photograph from a fixed object to a fluid image. The resulting 'algorithmic image' is itself only a potential visual — called into action by hardware and rendered through software. As such, it is able to be adjusted at will and poured into new spaces with ease. The outcome is the reproducibility of the image, the potential for infinite visual versions, and increasingly atomised photographic works.

Post-photography 'dissolves the notions of originality and ownership' while at the same time, the 'internet

35
When I speak about post-photography, I am not referring to changes regarding resolution, advances in lens technology or speed of image transfer, but fundamentally challenging assumptions and principles about photography that have remained with us, relatively unscathed, since the 19th century (regarding reproducibility, decisive image capture, the still photograph, materiality and the shape and function of the camera).

‘The book, with its genuinely creative potential, comes from the depths of the analogue age, and yet it is no contradiction that digital culture is arguably the most important resource for the new photobook culture, in a twofold sense: first, as a technical and communicative instrument by which the stimulation and production, distribution and circulation of books are accomplished; second, as a medium that, with the hyper presence of images, whether liberating or alienating, poses a challenge to the presence of photographs in the book.’ (Hagner 2020, 409)

‘The book is really the ideal format if you want to explore how to manipulate the conversation between images ... When I present a spread to you, you can only look at those two images that I have on that double-page spread. So I’m kind of forcing the viewer to look at just those images and try to figure out what it’s all about.’ (Eman Ali)

gives artworks a fluidity far greater than that of existing channels' (Fontcuberta 2015, 7). There are clear benefits here, but also new complications for a post-photographic world: a fragile ecosystem of trust in which the image is treated with increased scepticism. The change is put succinctly in Camila Moreiras' conviction that an abundance of images 'is not an example of numerical bounty but of a saturation that dismantles visibility' and that 'the age of post-photography is one in which the accountability of an image is no longer based on its validity' (Moreiras 2017). Such revisions of the status quo are facilitated by the malleability of the image and the new networks that surround it. Perhaps best seen in apps like Instagram (stories) and Snapchat, which accentuate non-permanence, the phenomenon of the fluid and mobile image is present in almost all visual spaces, which are updated with ease and therefore outdated quickly. Where the book, exhibition, magazine or photo album holds images in a state of permanence and fixity, the same is far less common on screen.

↘ A spread from Eman Ali's *Succession* (2019). Image courtesy of the artist.

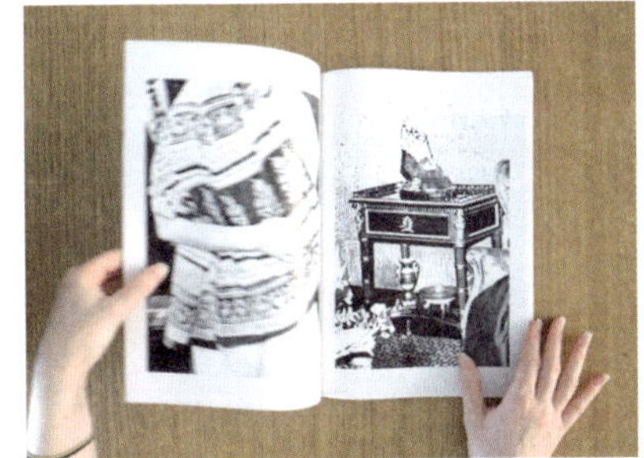

This poses new questions for the photographer. An emphasis on the immediacy of the image and its ability to float in different spaces presents new options in the dissemination of work, but consequent difficulties for those seeking to increase the longevity of works and retain control of a viewing environment. For many, the revised landscape of photography removes barriers and opens up a fluidity of working with images and other media in new ways, whereas for others, it symbolises the degradation of the medium or even, its death.[36] When images are moveable digital artefacts cascading into different screens in distant locations at different times, what experience can the photographer create for the viewer? Some have turned to arcane processes like tintype, ambrotype and cyanotypes in order to re-tether the photograph to materiality and aura in a manner that could be

36
For a while in the early 21st century, photography's death was announced regularly, so much so that Jörg Colberg produced a tongue-in-cheek chart to illustrate the likelihood of 'photography is dead' conversations that mirrored the US terror-threat level chart (2011).

considered part of an 'in real life' fetish (Jurgenson 2012), while others see possibilities in the book.

The photobook counters the fluidity of the image and its increasing temporality and de-territorialised nature. It offers a marker or point amidst an image-oriented life. The medium can be seen as a physical intervention into a scrolling mass of images[37] and an object with a 'sense of unhurried conclusiveness', allowing the reader to pause and reflect (Ludovico 2012, 30). The printed image in the book reverses the characteristics of what Hito Steyerl calls the 'poor image', which transforms 'quality into accessibility', 'contemplation into distraction' (Steyerl 2012, 32), and for photographers, is that object that will ensure 'that their artistic statement will remain unchanged, wherever and whenever their book is read' (The PhotoBookMuseum, 2014:18).

The finality of the page and the fixity of the book are great allies to photographers, in that they not only allow makers to determine the medium of presentation, but also provide a controllable, receptional device for the viewer.[38] Photographers are able to construct a book so large it demands that the reader sit down at a table, or so small and thin that it encourages a flick through on the train or bus. It should be no surprise, then, that the photobook has become an integral part of many photographers' practice. To produce a photobook is not only 'plain exciting', but an 'indicator of success' (Himes and Swanson 2010, 2) and an 'astute career move' (Badger and Parr 2004, 9).

The worth of the post-millennium siting[39] I have undertaken here is subtle but significant. It is of course quite possible to see the contemporary photobook only as a product of its makers, or to locate it only within a discourse of art (and photographic) history, but doing so provides a limited view. By acknowledging how the photobook exhibits characteristics of the post-digital, and challenges the fluidity, hyper-presence and

37
Moritz Neumüller suggests that: 'The book as an object will always be the way the author wanted it to be. If I send an image to your phone, the image will show in the way your phone wants it to show. The apparatus will decide how my image will look on your phone. But if I give you a book, the photograph will be in the way that I, the maker of the book, wanted it to be' (Vanthuyne & Neumüller 2017).

38
In this process the photographer is also able to accentuate the gap between the amateur and professional, one that is becoming increasingly opaque. This gap emerges because while publishing has to an extent been democratised, there are still barriers to entry in cost, skill and dissemination that replicate those in the gallery world. Thus, while a photobook or gallery exhibition is no more valid a presentation strategy than the use of a website, it carries with it a connotation of 'prestige' (Amak Mahmoodian) and authenticity, seen to 'embody wisdom in a way that the unstable electronic text does not' (Brigitte Frasse in Wirth 1995, 143–4).

abundance of the image in a post-photographic world, we may better understand not only the growth of the medium, but also what it provides in experience for those who engage with it. This knowledge can help to interrogate how the medium serves its makers and in turn how their choices in production influence the experience of reading and access to the book itself ('Photobooks & access'). Holding a mirror to our medium in this way is ultimately intended to support a more critical and pragmatic environment in which the photobook can be a vital asset in communicating urgent political, social and ecological issues to which photography bears witness.

↳ Notes

Though there has been much literature accompanying the photobook's acceleration in the post-millennium, there are fewer writings that deal with the phenomenon itself. Elisabeth Shannon's essay *The Rise of the Photobook in the Twenty-first Century* (2010), Bernard Yenelouis' *No Center, No Periphery* (2013), Doug Spowart's *The Photobook: Everyone a Publisher?* (2015a) and Oliver Cablat's writing in *Market? What Market?* (Tuminas and Neumüller 2017) are notable exceptions. There are additional writings that touch upon, rather than focus on, the influences of the photobook's rise found in Aperture's *PhotoBook Review* and many introductions or essays that populate books on books and exhibition catalogues. Interviews with publishers and photographers are another place to turn — Lesley Martin's conversation with LensCulture gives a good sense of the photobook landscape (LensCulture 2017).

There are an increasing number of resources to support the reader in encountering the post-digital, but the

39
In the coming chapters, more is done to contextualise the contemporary photobook in relation to the makeup and discourse of the photobook community ('Photobooks & community') and histories of publishing intent ('Photobooks & intent'). This approach will create a more holistic account of the contemporary medium that builds on this chapter's remit to establish a connection with the enormous technological changes that have swept through life and work in the last 20 years.

post-digital research issue of *A Peer Reviewed Journal About* is still a great beginning and includes Florian Cramer's thorough introduction *What is Post-digital?* (2014). Sy Taffel's *Perspectives on the Postdigital* (2015), Kim Cascone's *The Aesthetics of Failure: 'Post-digital' Tendencies in Contemporary Computer Music* (2000), Christiane Paul's *From Immateriality to Neomateriality* (2015), Lotte Philipsen's *Who's Afraid of the Audience?* (2014) and Caroline Bassett's *Not Now? Feminism, Technology, Postdigital* (2015) will introduce some different views and complexities to readings. Then, for a more focused look at the impact on print and publishing, *Post-digital Print: The Mutation of Publishing Since 1894* by Alessandro Ludovico (2012) and *Code-X: Paper, Ink, Pixel and Screen* (Aldred & Waeckerlé 2015) are both invaluable.

With the post-photographic in mind, Joan Fontuberta's *The Post-photographic Condition* (2015) and Camila Moreiras' *Joan Fontcuberta: Post-photography and the Spectral Image of Saturation* (2017) are useful texts. Going further, Nina Vestberg's *There is no Cloud: Toward a Materialist Ecology of Post-photography* (2016) and Haidy Geismar's *Post-photographic Presences, or How to Wear a Digital Cloak* (2016) introduce other concepts within the messiness of the post-photographic. Finally, for some broader thinking about the digital network, arts and the image, Hito Steyerl's *The Wretched of the Screen* (2012), Omar Kholeif's *You are Here — Art After the Internet* (2014) and the writing of Joanna Zylinska may be supportive beginnings.

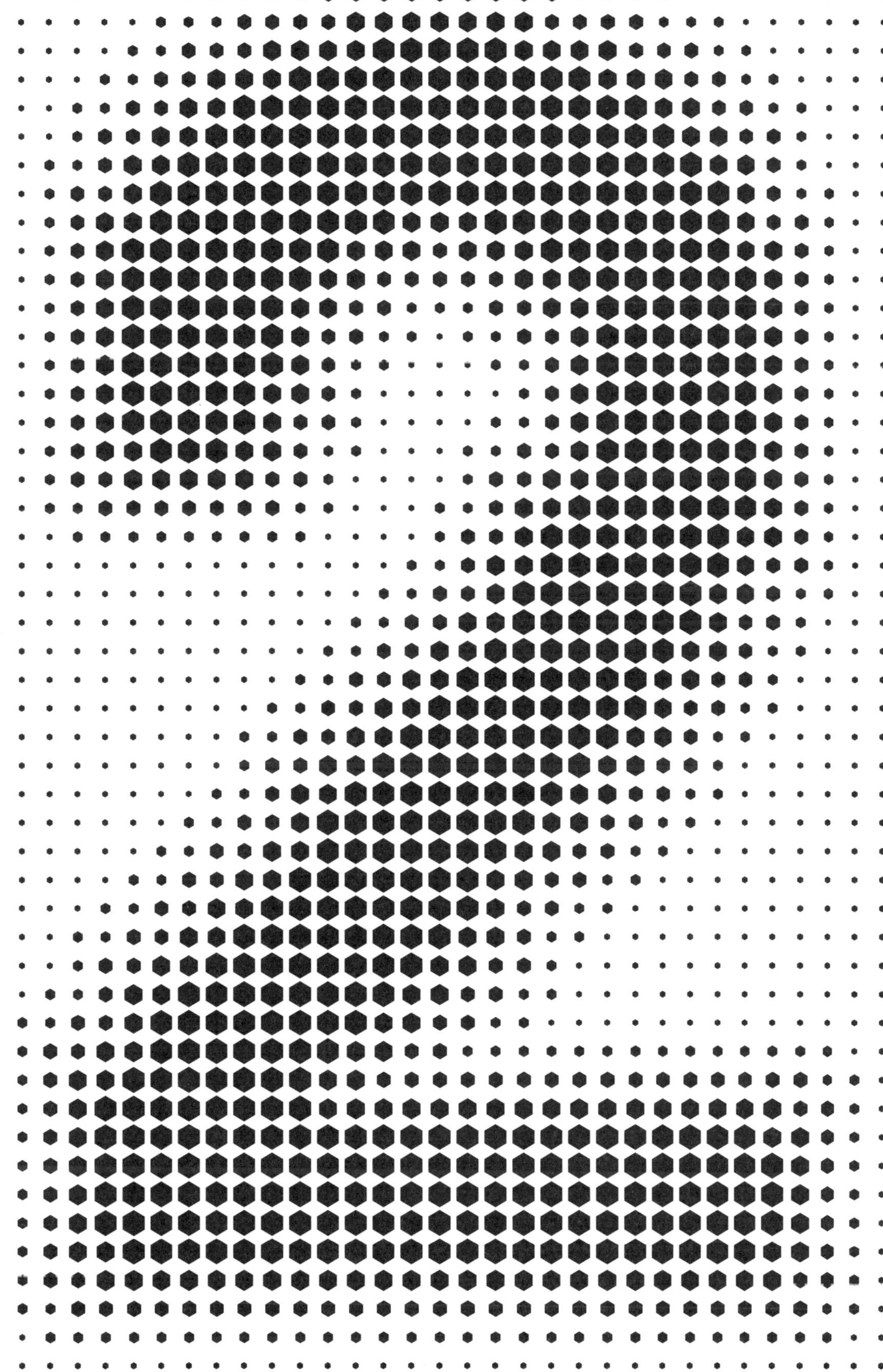

Photobooks & Community

As a medium of convergence — between the haptic and semiotic, between image, text and space — the photobook is also a meeting place for fields of practice. It is an intersection and potential interchange for the designer, printer, photographer, publisher, bookseller and, of course, readers in all their guises. With this foundation, a varied community constructing diverse and robust conversations could be expected, but it is not always forthcoming. Instead, the photobook can be seen as a medium that privileges making above other aspects of publishing, and has adopted a production-focused discourse. This occurrence helps to furnish a thriving yet insular era in which other makers form the primary audience for new publications.

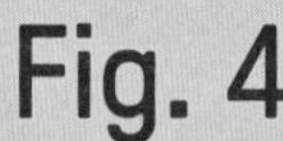

Professional identification of respondents (178*) to the photobook reading survey[43]

* Many respondents identified several professions, an indicator of our increasingly fluid and portfolio-oriented working lives

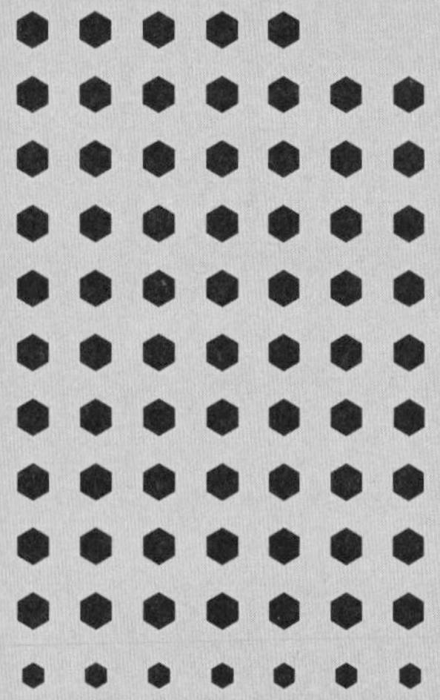

82 Photographer

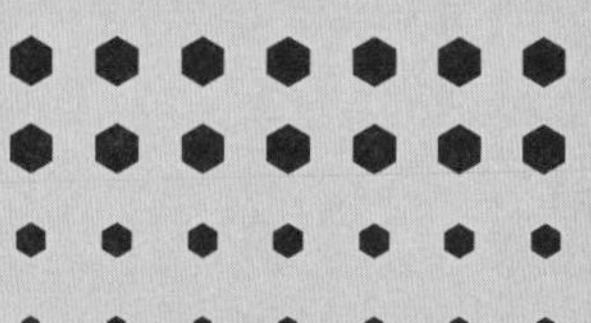

28 Photography teacher (or related subject)

18 Designer

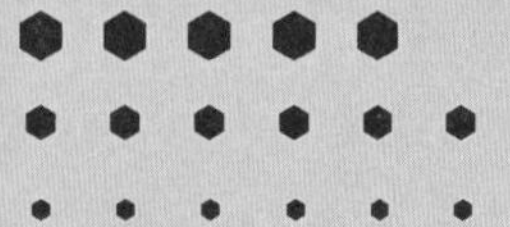

17 Curator

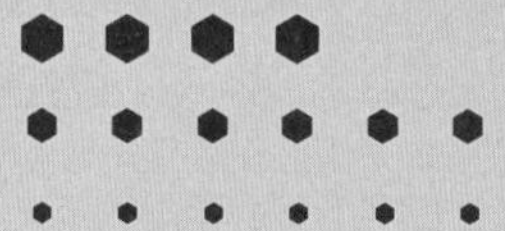

16 Writer

17 Publisher

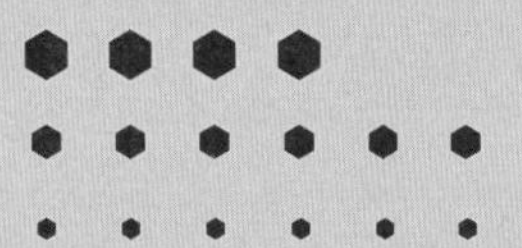

16 Photography Student

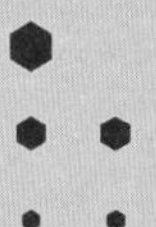

5 Editor

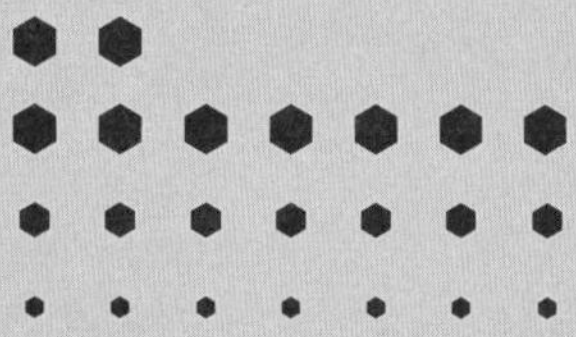

23 Other Creative Professionals

↳ A community of makers

Since the swell of activity charted in 'Photobooks & the post-digital' began in the mid-to-late noughties, little discussion has been given to the participants and producers of the numerous events, works, awards and institutions that coalesce around the photobook. There have been several suggestions of a cult-like landscape (Bush 2016) and frenzied characteristics of the circus (Martin 2014), but these alone have not managed to open a discussion around what can be learned from the demographic of those making or consuming photobooks.[40] Nor have they been able to interrogate how the way in which the medium is spoken about may impact its form. Here, I look to remedy this by first charting the makeup of the photobook community, as well as key aspects of its discourse, and subsequently theorising their impact on the medium and its perception.

In support of this agenda, in 2015 I undertook a large survey of those in the photobook community,[41] a section of which asked whether individuals had relationships to the photobook in a professional capacity. The results (see figure 4), which set the scene for this chapter, are telling of a body of people who, much like the photobook itself, are led by photography. In fact, those sitting outside the trio of photographer, designer and publisher whom I have termed the 'makers' are a minority, and even smaller (20%) are those who indicated that they were not involved professionally in the creative industries at all.[42]

Alone, this account of professional identification is interesting, but in combination with other responses regarding photobook production, dissemination and the feeling of belonging to the photobook community, it is aided in building more compelling narratives. One of the most striking is to see that over 70% of those surveyed were involved in making or disseminating

40
For clarity, two definitions from the glossary:

The photobook ecology: A term borrowed from Daniel Boetker-Smith (2015, 24), used to refer to the community, events, discourse, retail and products that construct and react to the photobook.

The photobook community: A group of individuals who coalesce around the contemporary photobook in fairs, festivals, blogs and social-media spaces, as well as constructing the medium itself in book publishing.

41
All 178 respondents to the survey were following a photobook-specific account, The Photobook Club, on social media.

42
Interestingly, of these individuals not identifying in the creative industries, almost half are still involved in some way in the production of photobooks.

← 43
Provided in two languages (English and Spanish), and available digitally online, the survey, like much activity in the photobook ecology, must be acknowledged as geographically skewed. The majority of respondents came from Europe, with clusters in North America and Australasia. Thus the conclusions drawn should not be assumed to speak of a global photobook, for its situations are unique and can be informed by national, regional and even highly localised forces.

photobooks. What's more, of this group, 77% considered themselves a part of the photobook community, compared to only 40% who were not involved in making or disseminating photobooks — the first strong indication of a maker-centric community.

- 66% of respondents identified as being involved in the production of photobooks and 37% identified as being involved in the selling or dissemination of photobooks (as a shop owner, writer/reviewer etc.).

- Of the respondents who are involved in the selling or dissemination of photobooks, 89% are also involved in the production of photobooks.

- Within the combined respondents involved in production or dissemination of the photobook, 77% considered themselves a part of the photobook community, and of these same individuals, 84% share thoughts on the photobook publicly.

- Of the individuals who did not identify as being involved in the production or dissemination of the photobook, 40% considered themselves part of the photobook community and 62% share thoughts on the photobook publicly. This makes the visibility of such contributions in relation to the makers only 24%.

By way of testing the validity of these findings, we can compare them with another data set. In 2019, Ivory Schellekens undertook the task of compiling all the year's 'best photobook' lists into one meta-list (2019). It is a fascinating resource and one that further evidences what has been seen so far. In a total of 132 lists, which included 251 contributors, 59% were makers (photographers, publishers or designers with a strong showing of the former) and only 4% were not overtly related in a professional capacity to photography. The majority of those who comprise the remaining 37%

were photobook collectors, photobook bloggers, festival organisers, photography writers and photography curators. This comparison confirms not only the prevalence of makers and those involved in the dissemination of photobooks, but also the resulting high visibility of their views.

What we see here is something that is far from unique to the photobook: even in fields populated by non-corporeal products, making is still often at the top of a community's hierarchy. In 2015, Debbie Chachra, a scientist and biological infrastructure professor, wrote an account of creation-focused tech-culture, in which there is an 'identity built around making things — of being "a maker"' and a 'widespread idea that "People who make things are simply different (read: better) than those who don't"' (2015). For Chachra, the democratisation of access through linked digital technology, the ability to make, has simply continued a hierarchy of making over not making.

We could describe the contemporary photobook, then, as a photographer's medium, and doing so would be supported by one of the most frequently cited interventions in the field — the three-volume history of the photobook by Martin Parr and Gerry Badger. In Volumes I and II, which were published before the rise of activity seen in 'Photobooks & the post-digital', there were a number of calls to think of the photobook as central to photography, and an explicit declaration in Martin Parr's preface to Volume II that their perspective is 'the viewpoint of the photographer' (Badger and Parr 2006, 4). Parr suggests that 'photographers learn more from other photographers' books than from any other source' (2006, 4) and that as a result, those most keen to engage with the medium are other practitioners 'hungry for new ideas' (2006, 8).

↳ A contributive discourse

The storylines gathered from my own survey, and supported in Schellekens' work, present a community that is oriented around production both in its demographic, and in the visibility and dominance of the maker's voice in discourse. It is proof in part of the value that the medium holds for those working with photography who may seek a more permanent, fixed or grounded home for images (see 'Photobooks & the post-digital'), but there are other nuances to be explored.

Since this is a community whose discussions take place in online spaces and via physical publications and events, it is not possible to listen in to all conversations. We are, though, able to look at representative textual discourse from a distinct space in which many members of the community participate. For this, I look to two large Facebook groups (Flakphoto Books and PhotoBooks) for data collection. With over 10,000 members each, they are what Howard Rheingold would call 'social aggregations' (1993, 3) and represent a significant portion of the digital space of the photobook.[44] In number, they account for the most concrete gathering of the photobook community — an ideal place in which to see how the photobook is discussed and framed.

What is apparent in an analysis of these spaces, is an absence of conversation, though this is not to say that there is an absence of activity. Both Facebook groups are populated by a great volume of posts — a regular stream of activity — but when seen closer there is little beyond the initial contribution of content. Evidence is available in considering the top 50 posts on these pages on a given day during this research: 4 November 2016. The table presented in figure 5.a. shows the total number of members of the group on this day, how many of the top 50 posts were shared from other Facebook locations (thus not an original contribution

44
'Social media is the communication vehicle of choice [for the photobook community] and participants in the photobook network are driven to frenetically seek updates, reviews, new releases, posts about their books and the latest gossip through social media channels' (Spowart 2015b).

Shares, comments and promotion across 50 posts in photobook-specific digital spaces.

Fig. 5.a

2016

Group	Members	Comments	Shared posts	Promotional posts
FlakPhoto Books	10,266	3	31	30
PhotoBooks	11,639	39	19	35

Fig. 5.b

Shares, comments and promotion across 50 posts in photobook-specific digital spaces.

2021

Group	Members	Comments	Shared posts	Promotional posts
FlakPhoto Books	13,038	46	22	46
PhotoBooks	14,658	34	25	45

of content to the group), how many of these 50 posts were promotional in nature, and how many comments, in reply to a posting, were present across these top 50.[45]

I undertook the same exercise in 2021 (see figure 5.b.). In this data, membership had increased, and so too had the number of promotional posts. Some of these posts are links to reviews that their authors are sharing, and a handful are to workshops or festivals in which the poster is involved, but the vast majority are photobook sellers and photobook makers. Comments in one group were also up, but still averaged less than one per post. There is unlikely to be much conversational exchange when there are fewer or equal comments to posts, and many of these posts are directing an audience to a shop, gallery or professional website.

What we are witnessing is not the result of the groups' mission; in fact, this analysis could be seen as counter to what they set out to do.[46] Their statements of purpose are illustrative of a larger trend towards contribution and away from critique and conversation. The result is that groups like these replicate the format of the fair or festival — they are spaces for sharing (what has been made), selling (what has been made) and promoting (what has been made). Exchange of ideas and goods may be occurring for many makers in private spaces, but since these potential exchanges lack visibility, they stand little chance of progressing a critical discourse directly — precisely why change in spaces like this will be slow.

The phenomenon seen here of contribution without conversation is difficult to untangle from an omnipresent interest in the new and the next. In the spaces of the contemporary photobook, little room is given to publications of a decade prior,[47] and much is made of emerging talent and new finds. Bruno Ceschel of Self Publish, Be Happy (SPBH) suggests that this may be due to an 'induced appetite' created by increasingly

45
Promotional posts were those that highlighted books for sale, or photobook events in which the poster has a vested interest. This includes bookshop or gallery workers posting about new books in their collections, as well as designers, writers, publishers and photographers (the makers), linking to publications in which they have been involved.

46
Flakphoto Books' 'about' page: 'Hello! This group is for people who love photography books. Feel free to promote your personal book projects, sell a book that needs a new home or simply recommend the titles you've been enjoying. All are welcome. Join us!' (FlakPhoto Books 2019).

PhotoBooks' 'about' page: 'This is a virtual space to share everything related to photography books! Here you will find posts on photobooks, links to reviews, blogs, photobook meetings, interviews, book publishers and more. Do post about your favourite photobooks and personal projects and, the most important, get inspired and enjoy the wonderful world of beautiful photography books!' (PhotoBooks 2019).

47
There are some important exceptions to note here, like Jeffrey Ladd's Errata Editions (he now runs 4b4 blog, which similarly leans away from the new), 10x10 Photobooks' reading rooms and Anabella Pollen's *Flea Market Photobook* series in *Source* magazine.

popular university classes that ask students to make books, and the decline of small galleries that may once have been the place in which to see new practitioners and their work. We could add to these factors the hugely popular online blogs that in the late noughties and early teens were creating a regular stream of content relating almost exclusively to new books. The Indie Photobook Library, the Independent Photobook, Self Publish, Be Happy and Alec Soth's book selfies on The Little Brown Mushroom blog all fed into the photobook community. Seldom did any look at works that were not new, and when there has been such a bounty, it is hard to see why they would have done.

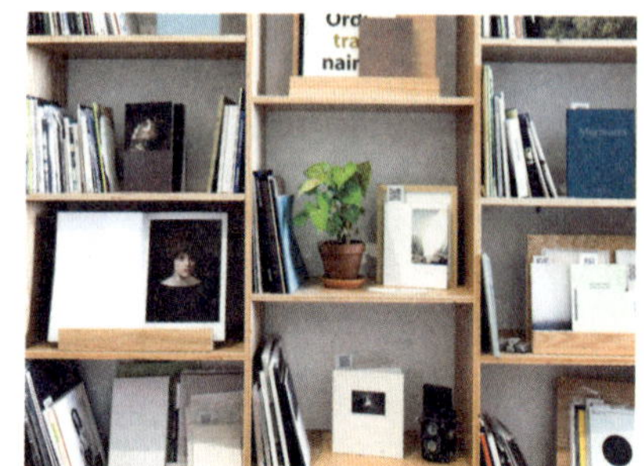

A pop-up Indie Photobook Library event at Conveyor Arts, 2012. Image courtesy of Conveyor Studio.

The networked technology seen in 'Photobooks & the post-digital' also plays a considerable role in accentuating the new. The structure of such technologies privileges new content to maintain visibility and interest, while the less overtly energetic and more complex that garner little in the way of quantifiable support (a share, a like, a retweet), sink to the bottom. We need only read about data-driven digital labour, or spend time with Rachel Maclean's dystopian *Again, Again and Again* (2016), to see how contributive action is consistently and covertly encouraged through networked and social technologies. In Jodi Dean's writing on communicative capitalism, the effect that our relationship with technology can have on placating and nullifying action is expounded thoroughly, offering an interesting perspective with which to view the contributive nature of photobook production and conversation.

Dean proposes that in a new political landscape, technological fetishism and a belief in the merit of abundance[48] contributes to a disconnect between action and results (2009, 19–48). She notes that contributing to a discourse feels positive, but has little bearing on action, policy and change. While Dean refers to the expression of perspectives on the internet, we can

48
'The internet enables millions not simply to access information but to register their points of view on websites and blogs, to agree or disagree, to vote, and to send messages. Communications, media, and information enthusiasts point to this abundance of messages as an indication of the democratic potential of networked technologies' (Dean 2009, 26–7).

think not only of the many online contributions referred to on prior pages here, but also the corporeal events and meetings that are facilitated and distributed via the internet, factors that encourage and highlight more makers than ever before who are working in the photobook form. The result is the appearance of a healthy, lively and successful discourse, but one that loses specificity and intent.

Purpose is central to Dean's critique of political discourse.[49] In her example regarding the war on terror, it is clear what the purpose of contributions is: the revising of policy, or recognition and debate with the official sphere of politics. The contribution of content in this example, whether the signing of petitions, sharing of posts or use of hashtags, makes senders feel as though they are doing good — that they have, through technology, been able to voice their opinions in a democratic manner and that these opinions, part of a groundswell, will be heard and responded to. Extrapolating Dean's critique to the photobook highlights potent parallels.[50] The newness, abundance and promotion of the photobook build a collective sense of a healthy and successful medium whilst losing individual specificity and worth. The apparent vitality of the medium does not transfer to the vitality of an individual book.

↳ A critical discourse

We might expect to find more focused and critical conversations in the many photobook reviews that populate pages of magazines, blogs and other digital platforms, but in reality many of these spaces often perpetuate the contributive discourse seen so far, albeit in a different guise. Photobook collector and writer David Solo suggests that the 'objective structured criticism of photobooks is still very immature' (Solo and Chiochetti 2020) in what feels like an echo of Johanna Drucker's introduction to the 2004 edition

49
It is also significant in *Photobooks &*, forming the core of my exploration in a series of lineages I present in 'Photobooks & intent', as well as featuring in 'Photobooks & the future'.

50
Applying a political critique as opposed to an art-historical or conceptual one is a statement of intent for the contextualised use of the photobook that can be amplified beyond an insular community, beyond esoteric discussions and beyond an emphasis on production.

of *The Century of Artists' Books*, in which she highlights the lack of critical engagement ten years after the often-cited book was first published (2004, iix). I would agree, and note that often in reviewing it is safest to write about the known quantities of a book — its physical construction, subject matter, photographic process, sequence and design, which leads us to overlook the murkier waters of its reception, worth, merits and flaws.

As a result, the review has become a space of recognition, in which a specific photobook is placed within a structure that tends towards the location of the work in relation to its media (photography and the photobook) and peer counterparts.[51] Such perspectives are vital as an aspect of critique, and construct a supportive environment for photobook making, but seldom ask questions of the role of the work in the world. While the artistic contextualisation of a photobook is a form of critical discourse, it is one that is likely to solidify the limitations of the medium within a restricted community, not look to extend and adjust its reach.

The issues we face in a narrow employment of considered criticism is akin to that with which the more established artists' books community has been wrestling for decades. In the preface to the indispensable *Artists' Books: A Critical Anthology and Source Book*, Dick Higgins highlights the need for criticism 'if the audience for artists' books is to continue to grow, if they are to reach a larger public' (1985, 12). Higgins' plea for criticism that would locate practice in a broader context, giving 'continuity with other times and cultures' (12) has been answered sporadically, though a change may well be in the air given the 2021 *Contemporary Artists' Books Conference* in the New York Art Book Fair, which took as a core tenet the need to 'make book art criticism more visible and more valuable' (Center for Book Arts 2020). As part of the Center for Book Art's *Manifesto for New Book Art Criticism*[52] is a

51
More discussion of the readings that form these reviews is given in 'Photobooks & the reader'.

52
Among the goals for a new approach to criticism, the Centre for Book Arts lists the necessity to acknowledge that 'the way we tell the history of book art needs to be expanded', to 'demystify artist books and make them more accessible' and to 'encourage dialogue in book art in as many forms and forums as possible' (Centre for Book Arts 2020).

recognition of the need to train and support individuals to achieve such goals (and some tangible activities to aid this). It is something from which photobook criticism could benefit greatly.[53]

Naturally, it will depend on each reader's position and perspective as to whether they deem the current discourse adequate in developing the medium beyond its current audience, or indeed if this is an aspiration for which criticism can be an ally. I posit that without a more robust discourse to sit alongside our existing activity, the photobook will not be supported in reaching its full communicative potential. It is a view that shares qualities with Melissa Miles' articulation in 2010:

> 'Curiously, contemporary critics and curators tend to focus on the books' formal characteristics such as design, paper stock and reproduction quality, or the historical importance of the photographs that are reproduced in the books, rather than their particular epistemological or ontological implications' (Miles 2010).

In addressing this gap, we should recognise the difficulty of critical writing and a lack of training in the area, but must reflect on how maker-centrism in our community also creates a space in which adopting a more critical position may be uncomfortable. As Corina Reynolds, part of the team constructing the aforementioned manifesto, notes, 'almost everyone who writes about books is a maker' (Printed Matter 2021b). The same is true in the photobook community, and as Bruno Ceschel points out, in such a small community, who would want to criticise a neighbour?[54] There are exceptions, but the voices to which we have often turned for their reflections on books are makers, or else are firmly within the ecology of the photobook and photography — leading to 'photobook criticism about photography or about where photobooks are important and the photographer's importance'

53
Lesley Martin: 'I do think we've lost a lot of the ability to write about photobooks and I don't mean within the photobook community, I mean at large. It's one of the barriers, I think, to getting reviews. People are intimidated by writing about photobooks; that's a problem.'

54
Bruno Ceschel: 'Perhaps it's because there's no appetite for it and maybe because we're too small a community to actually go after each other ... to be a critic and take a critical approach. It's always much more towards acknowledgment. Maybe it's the beauty of the small community — like living in a village. Who in the village would want to go to the square and criticise a neighbour?'

instead of 'situating [photobooks] in a large cultural context' (Tate Shaw). When this is combined with a contributive discourse, it is perhaps inevitable that the medium should have found itself in an increasingly contained and constrained network.

↳ Insularity and audience

For some, the very niche-ness of our medium is something rather attractive. Makers may like the small community setup in which they have the opportunity to be heard by others and where it is 'more likely they will get their work shown' (Sarah Bodman). There is much to be said for this, with the security of an environment populated by making-oriented individuals providing a conducive space for the development of the photobook's visual language. However, there is a fine balance to strike, and currently, our photobook community may well be so occupied with the making and the production of new, experimental and esoteric works that we reinforce an exclusivity of the medium.[55] This would be an echo of Simon Cutts' reflections on the state of the artist's book in 1995, when he proposed that 'if the whole arena is predicated on artists rather than the books themselves, then we will have made it a mirror of the gallery world, rather than benefit from a medium that has no social boundaries, and can precipitate change' (2007, 89).

Michael Mack cites the term 'photobook' itself, and its proliferation, as a 'touchstone for a much bigger problem' in which there exists a 'ghetto' with everyone 'rallying around the photobook flag', which he sees as being a 'dead-end'. It is a sentiment found also in Lewis Bush's terming of the photobook community as a 'cul-de-sac',[56] with connotations of 'suburban conservatism', 'curtain twitchers' and a 'general closed-in-ness' (Bush 2016):

55
'The photobook industry is not a huge industry, and it often annoys me that instead of evolving out of the niche, everything is done to strengthen it' (Tommaso Parillo in Morel 2020, 55).

56
A term also used by Simon Cutts to describe the artist's book (2007, 88).

57 ↪
This was acknowledged even in the second volume of Martin Parr and Gerry Badger's history: 'there are more photographers chasing book deals, and while the audience for photobooks has clearly expanded, it has not expanded in equal measure to the numbers of photographers trying to publish their books' (Badger and Parr 2006, 8).

‘[A belief in the power and efficacy of abundance] covers over the way facts and opinions, images and reactions circulate in a massive stream of content, losing their specificity and merging with and into the larger flow of data.’
(Dean 2009, 26)

‘As a medium, it’s something that has such a large global possibility for drawing connections with people. And it just seemed unfair to the medium that it was only photographers talking about photography and only photographers buying photobooks.’ (Anshika Varma)

> 'We don't really engage with the fact that the world outside the photo book cul-de-sac generally isn't that aware or interested [in] what we do. That's partly because sure, the photo book is a relatively newly recognised medium, but I think part of it is also because most photo book makers don't make any serious steps to speak to that world. I often feel that we are the ones relegating ourselves to our obscure cul-de-sac with a sometimes unquestioning adherence to a medium which might be very beautiful and often very appropriate to the stories we want to tell and the ideas we want to share, but perhaps often isn't remotely appropriate to the audiences we sometimes think we want to speak to' (Bush 2016).

It is likely to be clear already to readers in our community who are making books or involved in their production and dissemination, that the audience for the medium is small[57] and book purchases are being made predominantly by friends, colleagues and other makers. As Laia Abril puts it clearly, 'the public is us' (Abril et al. 2015, 28).[58] This limited audience has elicited different reactions in my conversations with individuals in the field. Whilst all recognise the phenomenon, some see it as inevitable and palatable while others see it as something that must be challenged.[59] There are those for whom the medium's passively porous walls are sufficiently supportive to those inside, whilst not precluding external visitors. And there are those for whom there is merit in a more active engagement with an outside world that may be uncomfortable, and will require considerable activity. If not already evident, my argument is firmly for extending the photobook and challenging its insular position.[60] I posit that beside the benefits of the photobook as a tool for communicating with more diverse audiences, change is also needed to prevent the stagnation of our community, which requires new voices in order not to collapse in on itself.

58
A feeling I have encountered often in my research. Alejandro Acin concurs with Abril's statement: '[Those buying books] are mainly practitioners, publishers or designers. There's something that has always been clear in this community — they know their audience is their own community.'

Bas Vroege of Paradox Publishing has made the situation equally plain: 'What we do with photobooks — we sell them for ourselves, photobook lovers, makers and people involved. We pump 70–80% of sales around within our community' (Tuminas and Neumüller 2017, 11).

59
Michael Mack: 'The approach that the photobook world has to the market is that "We know one another, that's sufficiently large; we can play in this space and that's great, that's enough.' For me, it's just not. It's not enough.'

Sarah Bodman: 'Most of us, we're preaching to the converted because all the people who come to those events or fairs ... generally are there because they want to be there ... I don't know if that means your audience is more limited, but does everyone have to be into it?'

60
The insularity I speak of here will appear again in 'Photobooks & access', where I look at how production, resulting cost, and the increasing sophistication of the photobook may present multiple barriers to those outside our community.

Since it was necessary to establish in this chapter exactly who comprises the photobook community, and how they operate, it will be no surprise that there are limited resources in this area. Tiffany Jones' *Dynamics of the Photobook Market* (2019) is an exception, as is Daria Tuminas and Moritz Neumüller's *Market? What Market?* (2017). In addition, as a temperature check and broad view of the photobook community, it is worth consulting the photobook-specific editions of photographic magazines and journals: *YET* magazine (2020), *Source* magazine (2016), *The British Journal of Photography* (2015), *Photofile* (2016), *PDN* (2013) and *The PhotoBook Review* (2011–ongoing). Despite an absence of critical consideration of the influence of community, the nature of the photobook ecology as one that is often organised and presented in digital spaces, means there is a wealth of information available to be investigated — from the recurrence of certain figures in committees and judging panels to the formats, prices and aesthetics of books themselves. With this in mind, *Ethnography and Virtual Worlds: A Handbook of Method* (Boellstorff et al. 2012), *Netnography: Ethnographic Research in the Age of the Internet* (Kozinets, 2010) and *Digital Ethnography: Principles and Practice* (Pink et al. 2016) may all be handy companions.

In looking to better understand the process of making photobooks (and to an extent the desire to do so), the reader might turn to recent publications like *Self Publish, Be Happy: a DIY Photobook Manual and Manifesto* (Ceschel 2015), *Understanding Photobooks: The Form and Content of the Photographic Book* (Colberg 2017) and *Publish Your Photography Book* (Himes and Swanson, 2014). Looking closer at the act of making may be supported by engaging with craft theory or even thing theory, but as a starter, the updated version of David Gauntlett's *Making is Connecting:*

The Social Power of Creativity, from Craft and Knitting to Digital Everything is valuable (2018). In helping to understand my hesitance to embrace maker-centrism, I found Debbie Chachra's short essay *Why I am Not a Maker* (2015) an incredibly useful text and might thus suggest that it is read alongside some of the more maker-centric texts that inevitably dominate reading around craft, production and construction. Joshua Simon's *Neomaterialism* (2012), as well as some of the reading from 'Photobooks & the post-digital', can contribute to a more holistic account of our relationship to making in the post-millennium.

The insularity that emerged in this chapter speaks of the contemporary photobook, but Thomas Dugan's interviews with photographers in *Photography Between Covers* (1979) adds an intriguing historical perspective to some of what has been seen, in particular, A.D. Coleman speaking about edition size, audience and the role of the critic as an 'intermediary' (1979, 197). Clearly, Jodi Dean's writing in *Democracy and Other Neoliberal Fantasies* (2009) has been influential in this chapter, as has Pierre Bourdieu's *Photography: A Middle-brow Art* (1996),[61] both of which have more to offer than has been dealt with in these pages. The reader may wish to engage with the *Photobook Sessions* conference recording from May 2021, when it becomes available, in which a discussion of the role that critical writing plays in contextualising and supporting the contemporary photobook takes place — Tanvi Mishra's voice is particularly interesting given the content of this chapter.

Lastly, a separate discussion can be had around the frenzied search for, and presentation of, photobooks as the 'final frontier of the undiscovered', which is the photobook's historical canon (Badger and Parr 2004, 4). It would be illuminating to consider how much influence particular figures have had in forging chronologies of significance. It is possible to see canon-creation as

61 Originally published in French as *Un Art Moyen: Essai sur les Usages Sociaux de la Photographie* in 1965.

an elevation of lesser-known works, or alternatively as an exploration linked with market value and tinged with colonial tendencies.

Photobooks & Intent

The photobook was once seen in the interstices made between photography, artists' books, zines, archives and mainstream presses. Now it occupies its own defined space, with a production-oriented community and accompanying discourse that is often promotional and celebratory. This shift, capped by the adoption of the term 'photobook', provides an ease of connection between like-minded individuals, but belies the ontological roots of the medium. Thus, the photobook has become a representation of itself, untethered from historical photographic relationships with the page. By way of response, lineages of the photobook seek to reconnect with the purpose of publishing and provide a critical aid for the maker and critic.

↳ Unpacking the photobook

> 'It is now de rigueur for any photographer of ambition to make a book. Whether their primary arena is in the commercial studio, the war zone, or the art gallery, a successful photobook gives a considerable boost to a photographer's credibility' (Badger and Parr 2006, 7).

Under the banner of the 'photobook' we find a dizzying array of interactions between photography and the page. In design, production and content, the photobook is far from a homogenised medium. It spans in its physical body from the grand and tome-like, to the handmade and delicate, while in content it covers the breadth of life itself. A feature of the richness of the medium, this also reveals problems with the inadequacy of current photobook language, which impacts our ability for focused critical discourse. In attempts to counter this situation (or else understand it through documentation), there have been a number of propositions for taxonomies that break down the broad field of the contemporary photobook. Four of these suggestions are outlined over the next few pages and reflected upon for their ability to progress an understanding of the photobook that extends beyond intra-medium workings to consider how the book transports content and ideas to a readership. Put simply, how do taxonomies help to address the making public of publishing?

In early 2018, Jörg Colberg presented a taxonomy of the photobook on his popular Conscientious blog. Colberg's self-imposed remit was to look specifically at narrative forms, putting aside subject or production-oriented details to see 'how the books operate, how, in other words, the story is being told' (2018). Colberg proposes five types of photobook: catalogue, monograph, journalistic, lyrical and narrative dream (2018), some of which have additional sub-categories and all of which are accompanied by a description.[62] Colberg's taxonomy is a system that can be applied with relative ease — the clear summaries of the way in which the narrative operates mean I am able to quickly relate each to a book on my shelf. It captures some current trends in photobook narrative, and documentary storytelling in particular, very well. This taxonomy's precision (17 styles in total), as well as its concentration on the intricacies of the photographic sequence, however, position it firmly as an aid for makers (part of Colberg's remit) embarking on sequence construction, or those closely studying the form as art object.

Whereas Colberg looked at narrative separated from photographic content, Lesley Martin's *Invitation to a Taxonomy of the Contemporary Photobook* (2017, 11–14) is built around 'trends' and 'tracks' that accommodate subject matter. Her proposal is focused in its scope, looking to understand the 'recurrence of a particular set of ideas — a coalescing of new forms'. Thus, Martin is concerned with what the contemporary photobook features, and what form it takes. For her, there are three defining tracks: the 'Thematic track: The archive' – works that resonate with the 'preoccupations of the photography world at large' (11); the 'Narrative track: Photobook as puzzle' (12) – those books that 'eschew traditional organisational hooks and are organised neither chronologically nor as a clear progression from beginning to end'; and the 'Production track: Baroque form' (13), where Martin locates a range of books, from those challenging the physical parameters of the book itself, to, on the other end, books that engage 'with the smorgasbord of possibilities' in contemporary publishing. Martin's proposal, much like Colberg's, is easy to apply to books on the shelf, and achieves its purpose in identifying particular recurrences in sequence, design and construction.

Unlike the taxonomies of Colberg and Martin, Doug Spowart's A Spectrum: *Photobook to Artist's Book*

62
On the elliptical category (a subset of lyrical photobooks), Colberg writes:

'Elliptical storytelling involves omitting or withholding part of the events or aspects so that the viewer (or reader) will fill in the gaps. The gaps thus are not gaps in a literal sense (that would make the viewer stumble). Instead, the narrator relies on the viewer being able to provide the content, thus possibly allowing for narrative ambiguity' (2018).

borrows from, and borders with, an artist's book discourse[63] — looking to make connections with a world outside the photobook. At one end of Spowart's spectrum is the deluxe photobook, and at the other end, the artist's book and *livre d'artiste*, which incorporate photographic images. Comprised of nine colour waves, Spowart's spectrum is focused on process, publishing pragmatics and material factors, aided by descriptors:

> 'Printing techniques such as silkscreen, photoetching and gravure, inkjet, digital press and alternative imaging techniques like cyanotype.'
>
> 'Books engineered in ways that demand interaction, both through the visual senses but also through the haptics of handling and reading – the turning of pages.'
>
> 'Print runs may be small and limited or quite extensive ... of 1,000 copies or more' (Spowart, 2018).

Key to Spowart's proposal is its intention to 'bring visibility to the diversity of creative publishing' and acknowledge 'links with artists' books and zines that can enrich the discipline of the photobook' (2018). So, where Colberg is concerned with the operation of the sequence, and Martin is interested in highlighting key themes and trends in design and content, Spowart looks instead towards the mechanics and practicalities of photobook making in a broader context of arts publishing. Each of these proposals is successful in its aim to better understand the photobook through a taxonomic breakdown, and each presents for us a number of interesting questions to explore, but they operate primarily in a discourse of production and production study. Put differently, these three proposals alone do not offer aid for a consideration of publishing as a process of bringing a work to a given readership.[64] If we are to move towards an approach that foregrounds the function of the photobook in reaching

63
Spowart explicitly references and incorporates some of the language of Clive Philpot from his 1998 writing on the spectrum of works that sit within, and alongside, the artist's book (2012, 193–4).

64
Though it is only a brief portion of a larger piece, a lecture that Spowart gave on the Antipodean photobook does begin to deal with readership. Spowart groups together different 'tribes' of book makers and notes that some 'make books because they can', while others are 'creating books to distribute ideas and social comment' (Spowart 2019).

and engaging with readers,[65] we begin to find support in Philip Zimmerman's *Photo-bookwork Graphic-continuum Chart* (2016).

Zimmermann presents a spectrum with a continuous line of examples spanning from, on one end, the 'photography book' and on the other the 'photo-bookwork'. Alongside this runs a parallel spectrum of identifying characteristics like the adoption of a 'dustjacket', 'full page bleed' or 'creative use of white space'. This demonstrates a similarity with Spowart in the mechanics of the production of the photobook, but what differentiates Zimmermann's position is his insistence that intention contributes to the place of a work on the spectrum. He goes on to note the distinction between the re-presentation of work that is trying to promote a show, and the use of the book as an expressive medium for new work. This accent on intent shifts the location of critique towards the relationship between the makers' choices in publishing and their desires for the book. This is succinctly put in the closing remarks of the chart, in which Zimmermann takes aim at books that pretend to be something they are not:

> 'There are many books which use the external trappings of artists' books like fancy covers and production materials, but do not use the language or have the intent of an artist's book, nor do they exploit how books work as a medium except in a very simplistic way. (Many of Martin Parr's books are great examples of this. I think of dressed up books like this as sheep in wolves clothing. I like sheep and I like wolves, but in this case it's one species pretending to be another)' (Zimmermann 2016).

Zimmermann's chart was introduced at a symposium in 2016. and has since been located on the College Book Arts' Art Theory blog, where it is accompanied by additional contextualisation and a call for consideration of why the book is to be published. Zimmermann

65
A means of combating some of what is seen in 'Photobooks & community' and 'Photobooks & access' — a relatively insular audience for the photobook.

asks of the photobook maker 'what is it that you want to use the book for?', going on to highlight the fact that while 'the monograph does the job of promoting single photographs or bodies of work ... books are capable of much more' (Zimmermann 2016). Here, more than in the other spectrums and taxonomies proposed, I find a sentiment that resonates with this research and its remit to generate attention regarding publishing beyond the publication: not only making, but making public.

↳ Intent as a taxonomic tool

The intra-photobook definitions that we have just witnessed demonstrate an understanding that the photobook as a single term of unification can bring together, and hide, intricacies, complexities and nuances that could be vital to our critical analysis of the medium. Colberg, Martin and Spowart have sought comprehension and investigation from the position of art-criticism, whilst Zimmerman in his spectrum begins to move towards a consideration of the function of the photobook in the process of publishing, and the book as a text in the world that is aligned to particular intent.

What happens, then, if we bring the role of intent right to the centre of a taxonomy that looks to account for a wide variety of uses for the book, and employs intent as a guiding principle for categorising works?[66] This, I propose, would allow a more rigorous interrogation of photobooks and their connections with readers in a taxonomy of purpose. Adoption of this approach would not preclude discussions of aforementioned topics and use of other taxonomies, but would rather give critics and readers a context in which to discuss such intricacies as printing methods, with an eye to how it affects the ability of a publication and its contents to connect with a readership. In this way, it could be said that my proposal is not counter, but complementary – enriched by, and in turn enriching, companionable approaches.[67]

66
Some may wonder why Zimmermann's chart is not suitable already. Despite its suggestion of intent as separation between works on the spectrum, the intent is still narrow — between the recording of a body of work, the promotion of a show or an expressive publication showing new work. These, I would suggest, all fall within the narrow confines of the audience established in 'Photobooks & community'. In order to provide support for grasping the connections between a broader range of photobooks and their readers, a more inclusive and expansive approach is required.

67
In my proposed taxonomy, just like the four considered previously, there are omissions. Clearly, with an agenda to accentuate the purpose of publishing, other elements have been put to one side. Thus for many, considering several taxonomic approaches in reviewing works (pre- or post-production), would be valuable and provide a depth that none, on their own, can offer.

↳ Purpose-informed lineages

What is proposed over the coming pages is a taxonomy of *lineages* from which the contemporary photobook emerges. These lineages trace the photobook back to roots that are anchored in purposeful uses of the printed page. While the focus of these lineages is not historical, they do demonstrate how the photobook has proliferated not from nothing, but from a series of non-unified spaces of discourse and production. The three lineages, which will be addressed in order, are the lineage of the photographic book-photobook, the lineage of the artist's book-photobook and the lineage of the photo essay-photobook, all of which have contributed to, and are found within, what we now refer to as the contemporary photobook.

↳ The lineage of the photographic book-photobook

Photobooks that operate in the lineage of the photographic book-photobook are works that bring images together with a commonality that is often thematic, but could also be geographic or aesthetic. They may have been produced by one artist, in one location, or by many artists in many locations in different periods of time. The photographs in the photographic book-photobook may not originally have been made with the intention to be displayed in a bound codex, but, as per our working definition of the medium as a whole,[68] there is consideration of the book as output in the editing and sequencing of the work.

This lineage is one that can be traced back to the very first interactions of photography and the printed page, interactions that relied on the book as a container of images and one of the only ways in which to view images themselves. In the lineage of the photographic book-photobook, the content of the book is of primary interest to the audience and thus, the prevalence of

68
The photobook is a single or multi-authored, bound work with photography as its primary content. It is an expression of a unified thought, subject, position, location or time that has been constructed with awareness of the physical book as output.

‘The “photobook” label is increasingly used to designate a book’s aesthetic and market value to the exclusion of all other types of worth. This obscures individual books’ historical, cultural and ideological origins, obstructing our ability to assess the photographic book’s nature and value.’ (Shannon 2010, 55)

Fig. 6

The roots of the contemporary photobook in three lineages

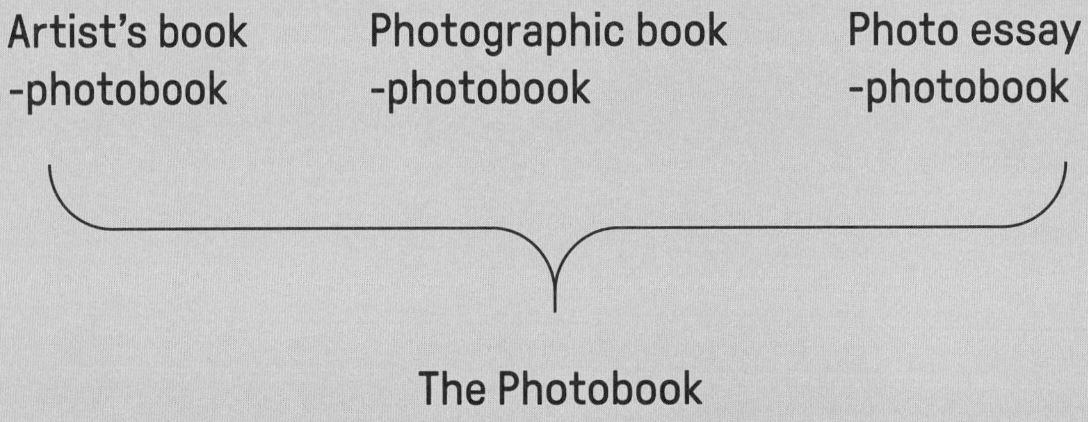

Artist's book -photobook

Photographic book -photobook

Photo essay -photobook

The Photobook

↴ *Walter Chandoha, the Cat Photographer* by Walter Chandoha, Brittany Hudak and David La Spina (2015). Image courtesy of Aperture and the Walter Chandoha Archive.

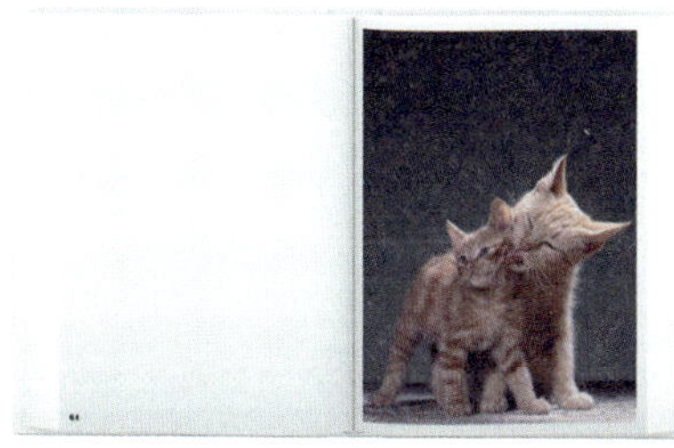

'travel ... landscapes ... ancient monuments and works of art' of which Gerry Badger and Martin Parr spoke in early photographic books (2004:16), are still highly visible in contemporary examples.

> Historical examples: *Observations* (Avedon and Capote 1959); *Ryurai Ryukyo 1954–1973* (Shisui 1974); *Faces of the 80s* (Levine 1987).
>
> Contemporary examples:[69] *Walter Chandoha, the Cat Photographer* (Chandoha, Hudak and La Spina 2015); *Trilogy* (Nan 2018), *Dawoud Bey: Seeing Deeply* (Bey 2018).

In this lineage, the purpose of publishing is to provide an assemblage, or experience, that is not available elsewhere. Thus, the photographic book-photobook is a presentational medium and ultimately, a container of work. Its function as a container in this lineage can be connected with the very earliest photobooks and swathes of highly influential publications, but it has also often meant that it has been excluded from contemporary conversations. The photographic book-photobook is less common in prize shortlists, is often excluded from definitions of the photobook, and at times is seen as a lesser version of the medium. This sentiment can be traced back to Alex Sweetman's description of Richard Avedon's and Henri Cartier-Bresson's publications as 'mere portfolios between covers' (Sweetman 1985, 187).

↳ The lineage of the artist's book-photobook

Works that operate in the lineage of the artist's book-photobook[70] can be considered primarily as personal reflections on the world, or an interrogation of medium (often both). While they may be produced in response to a global event or cultural phenomenon, the work is frequently the result of an individual

69
Here I have chosen books that would not be out of place in the photobook community's discourse, but we can also add to the above some books that are more overtly commercial or mass-market oriented:

Patterns of the Earth (Edmaier 2007); *Mountain High: Europe's 50 Greatest Cycle Climbs* (Friebe and Goding 2015); *An Opinionated Guide to London Pubs* (Gili and Curtis 2021).

70
As will be seen, the characteristics of the artist's book that I align with the photobook in this lineage, position the work primarily in an avant-garde art context. There is, though, a substantial history and discourse around the artist's book and its various subsets that focus on different defining features in content, production, distribution and even editioning. *Artists' Books: A critical anthology and Sourcebook* (Lyons 1985) and Clive Phillpot's *Booktrek* (2013) offer starting points for engaging with this conversation.

perspective, and rarely eludes to objectivity or uses such language as to suggest truths beyond the singular subjective.

> Historical examples: *Growing up Female: A Personal Photojournal* (Heyman 1974), *Silent Book* (Rio Branco 1997).

> Contemporary examples: *A Certain Kind of Energy* (Pongo 2013), *Be Happy!* (Samelot 2013), *Moisés* (Sancari 2015), *A Rock is a River* (Rochat 2017).

The lineage of the artist's book-photobook is one that when traced back does not emerge at the root of the artist's book itself, but rather what it became. Lucy Lippard reflected on this change in 2006 when she articulated that the artists' books she was seeing were not the 'idealistic, populist' publications she wished for, but rather were 'art, avant-garde art' and as such were not accessible to a broad public (Ault 2006). It is a transition noted also by Ermanno Rivetti, who highlights the benefits this brought for artists to experiment with the book form:

> 'As television and radio began to flex their muscles, artists' books were no longer adequate vehicles for political discourse... they became more conceptual, abstract and even more open to experimentation' (2012, 17).

This lineage, then, is one that is 'defined (and confined) by an art context' (Lippard 1985, 47). So it is that the artist's book-photobook shares a trait with publications like *Provoke* in Japan as a 'magazine intended for a restricted market with a common subset of interests, as opposed to general readers' (Vartanian 2009, 17),[71] or *Camera Work* periodical, with an audience that comprised the same people whose work was featured or who were submitting to the publication (Fernández 1999, 12).

71 Speaking about the Japanese photobook in the 1960s and 70s, Ivan Vartanian describes the audience for these works as relatively insular: 'A great deal of Japanese photo books functioned just short of a roman á clef, wherein only a closed circuit of readers was privy to the true core of a body of work' (2009, 12).

When considering purpose, the artist's book-photobook provides both a space of artistic freedom, and a platform for interrogation of the book as medium. The book affords makers an opportunity to explore their work in the confines (and possibilities) of the printed codex with control over sequence, scale, design, printing and so on, and in turn, this situation also encourages interrogation and exploration of the medium itself, such that the book becomes a second subject of the work. The photobook in the lineage of the artist's book-photobook can be distilled to an artwork and a vehicle for self-expression.

↳ Mariela Sancari's *Moisés* (2015). Image courtesy of the artist.

↳ The lineage of the photo essay-photobook

The influence of the photo essay is highly visible in the contemporary form of the photobook, 'enjoying a renaissance, in part because the book is an ideal vehicle' for documentary narratives (Colberg 2017, 38). The lineage of the photo essay-photobook is concerned with the world in which its authors and (importantly) its readers, are situated, often striving to inform, generate discussion, or encourage action. In short, this lineage connects with Johanna Drucker's remarks about the book as a vehicle for social change, which can provide 'a platform for social critique or as a means of advocating directly for specific policies' (Drucker 2004, 287).

This lineage can be aligned with the documentary tradition and the photo essay itself, which 'pioneered a new way of reaching and influencing an audience' (Webb, 2013:115),[72] but the purpose of publishing to witness and educate is not restricted to this form. Works with non-established readerships can also be included. This is a distinction that sets the lineage of the photo essay-photobook apart from that of the photographic book-photobook (with an audience that

72
In his taxonomy, when speaking about the photojournalistic photobook, Colberg makes the same connection with the history of visual journalism, stating that such books rely 'heavily on storytelling devices that were established during what we could call the golden age of the photojournalistic story (*LIFE* Magazine etc.)' (Colberg 2018).

is typically already interested in a given subject, theme or practitioner), and the lineage of the artist's book-photobook (with an audience already interested in the medium of the photobook itself).[73]

> Historical examples: *You Have Seen their Faces* (Bourke-White and Caldwell 1937), *Snow Land* (Hamaya 1956), *Viet Nam in Flames* (Dan and Hanh 1969), *Un Album di Violenza* (Oursler 1976),
>
> Contemporary examples: *Go No Go* (van Denderen 2003), *Concresco* (Galjaard 2012), *The Epilogue* (Abril 2014), *There are no Homosexuals in Iran* (Rasti 2017), *Woman Go No'Gree* (Oyarzabal 2020).

The work in this lineage could be a 'searing documentary photo essay crafted to affect social change' or may be constructed to 'tell a story about [a] local community' (Himes and Swanson 2014, 29). A concentration on connecting with an audience beyond those who may ordinarily seek out such narratives is key to the photo essay-photobook, and highlights the role of publishing in mobilising work. The purpose in this lineage, then, is for the photobook to act as vehicle and platform for the maker to communicate narratives about the world, to audiences that could be described as previously unaware of, or who do not possess an interest in, the subject of the book or medium itself. This lineage engages the photobook as a carrier of work.

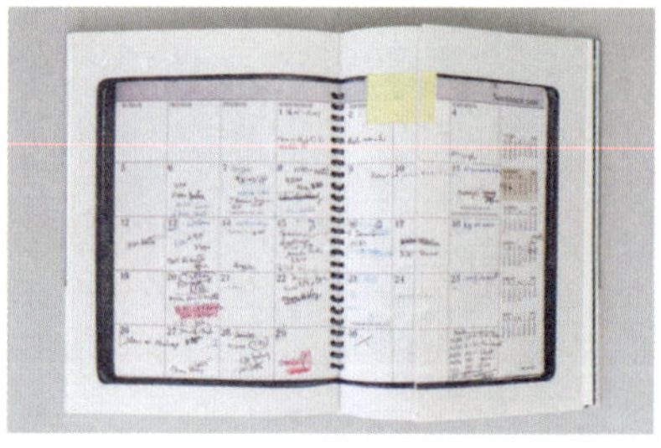

⌞ Laia Abril's *The Epilogue* (2014). Image courtesy of the artist.

It may be noted that edition size has not come into my discussion of lineages. It is a complicated subject, made more so by the general trend in current publishing towards smaller print runs, which makes historical comparisons more difficult. When we add to this the fact that a photo essay-photobook may well seek to speak directly to a particular local community readership comprised of hundreds, not thousands, and that artist's book-photobooks may be limited runs for a

73
This categorisation also allows for the inclusion of a diverse range of publications that in some locations will stand in opposition and counterpoint to ruling propaganda. For example, Horacio Fernández speaks about Latin American photobooks that have often been realised as defiant 'books of protest, denunciation, memory or independent journalism' (2011, 20).

‘I never really question the term “photobook” because it’s perfectly functional. I do very much think that a lot of publications that are in the SPBH collection, as well as the publications I do ... are much more in line with traditional artists’ books than photobooks. But this is more in terms of their form, and the reason for them to exist, for me as a publisher as well as the author of the book.’ (Bruno Ceschel)

Fig. 7

A condensed table of lineage

	Purpose	Function
Photographic book -photobook	To collate and present	As container
Artist's book-photobook	To explore, interrogate and promote	As artwork
Photo essay-photobook	To inform and educate	As carrier

small artistic community or experimental democratic multiples that retain an esoteric visual language and subject matter, the matter is muddied further. But, just as we might have difficulty in categorising some of the most well-known examples of the photobook,[74] these struggles are an example of how the products of taxonomy application are most significant in conversation and investigation, rather than result.

↳ The implications of lineage-oriented discourse

The three lineages of the contemporary photobook are presented in a condensed fashion in figure 7. In this distilled form, they show how, when we accentuate the purpose of publishing, we similarly accentuate different uses of the photobook. These uses are not fixed, but are indications of the need for specific critique. As an example, it would be unreasonable to admonish the makers of an artist's book-photobook for its niche references or elaborate and expensive production traits, since this is likely to have little impact on adjusting its readership, only enhancing it. On the other hand, it may be appropriate to level such a critique at photo essay-photobook makers who purport to raise awareness of a particular matter, or engage with broader public conversations, if they adopt the photobook only as artwork rather than carrier.[75] It is worth remembering here that intent is often connected with content, but that the two are not inseparable — a highly personal work could, should the makers intent align, operate in the lineage of the photo essay-photobook.

The choice to establish lineages here that are informed by a purpose of publishing, and not categories defined by production values, narrative construction, subject matter or aesthetics, owes a great deal to the historian John Tagg. Tagg's rethinking of the history of photography as the 'histories' of photography (1988) is a proposal that allows histories to be seen in the

74
It is worth acknowledging two book projects with which many readers will be familiar and may wonder where they fit into my lineages. Anna Atkins' *Photographs of British Algae: Cyanotype Impressions* (1843) and the book works of Ed Ruscha are both central to many discussions of the origins of the contemporary photobook. In the context of lineages, however, they are complex works. Atkins' publication can be seen in its form and content to sit at the emergence of the photographic book-photobook lineage, but its limited distribution – which is debated (Lubben 2019, 15) – would see it aligned with the artist's book-photobook. Conversely the content and language of Ruscha's works operate within the artist's book-photobook lineage but Ruscha's striving for democratic distribution and communication beyond the art world could place it in the lineage of the photo essay-photobook.

75
A carrier need not ignore its potential as artwork, and likewise, the photobook as container must still transport its content to a reader. The characteristics of which I have spoken are present to focus conversation on a primary goal in publishing, rather than to ignore all other aspects.

context of the spaces in which they operate.[76] While Tagg had weightier intentions than ours, and sought to challenge the institutional use and misuse of photography as a tool of power, the concept is one that has been instrumental in thinking about the defining, and application, of lineages. The use of lineages is designed to explore the actions and interactions of photobooks with the world: the maker's employment of the form as a functional medium to meet purpose. As such, lineages reject the study of the photobook as an isolated output in the vein of formalist[77] reading.

The three lineages that sit under the umbrella term 'photobook' are not intended to be terms that become widely adopted by the photobook community, or those on the periphery. Rather, it is hoped that the terms may help to bring into focus the purpose of publishing, and that this purpose may become a common ground for the maker, reader and scholar. In addition, the application of lineages highlights how the unifying photobook term is able to bring together, but also mask, a series of histories of purpose that could support the contemporary photobook's future.

With practicability in mind, textual accompaniments to a photobook may be the single biggest aid for those not directly involved in the production of a given work, in deducing its lineage. This method can be augmented with additional research in interviews, features and so on, but a focus on text that was produced in conjunction with a publication launch, I suggest, will be one of the clearest indicators. The following series of keywords, which are often found directly, or their connotation is suggested, in blurbs, press releases and other photobook metadata are aligned to particular lineages.[78] Extracts from blurbs of photobooks published in 2019 are included as examples:

- The photographic book-photobook: collect, present, display, assemble, thematic

76
'Photography as such has no identity. Its status as a technology varies with the power relations which invest in it. Its nature as a practice depends on the institutions and agents which define it and set it to work ... It is this field we must study, not photography as such' (Tagg 1988, 63).

77
Formalism does not take into account the manner or circumstances in which the work has been produced or received. Instead, it is considered as 'an autonomous object divorced from the specific circumstances of its creation and creator, and from the historical and social context of its reception' (Cook 1995, 130).

78
Here, much can be said about the tension between purposes that lineages can reveal. If a book that, due to its accompanying language, would be placed in the lineage of the photo essay-photobook is formed in a manner aligning with the artist's book-photobook lineage, does the inconsistency arise from the form of the book or its accompanying language?

Fig. 8.a

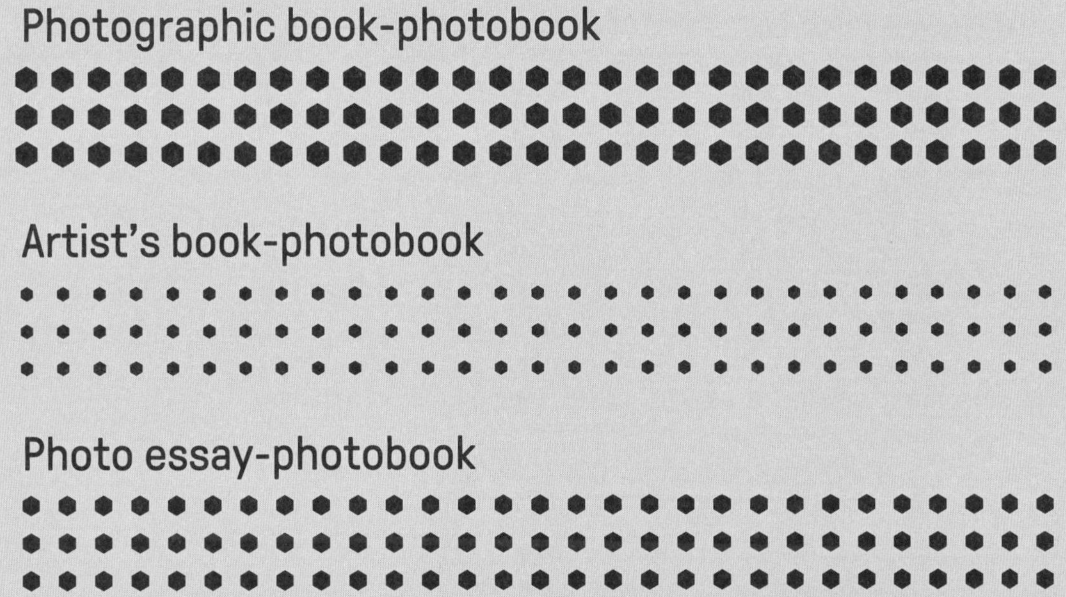

Photographic book-photobook

Artist's book-photobook

Photo essay-photobook

Fig. 8.b

Masking of lineages by the unified photobook term.

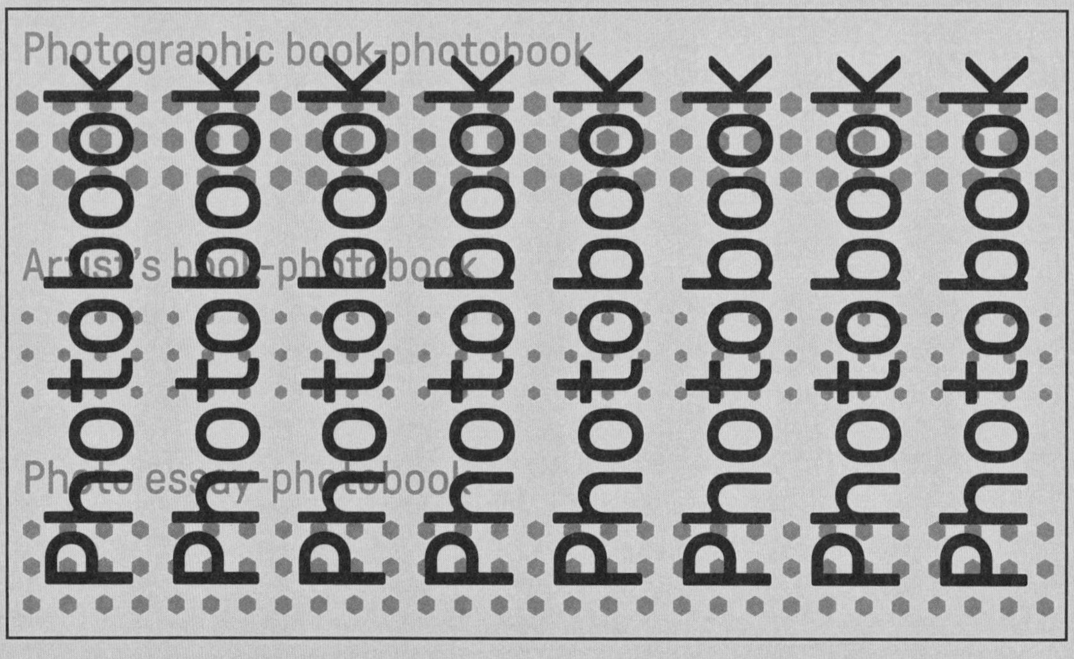

Ari Marcopoulos: Entropy (Marcopoulos and Sultan 2019): 'Ari Marcopoulos was born in Amsterdam in 1957 and moved to New York in 1980, at the height of the city's art scene. An artist, filmmaker, and photographer, his body of work includes portraits, street scenes, and landscapes from places as diverse as Tokyo, Lebanon, New Orleans, Brooklyn, and the California coast. His subjects have been musicians, celebrities, artists, and friends, as well as the anonymous denizens of the boroughs he has wandered.'

Antony Cairns: CTY (Cairns and Baker 2019): 'CTY brings together a large selection of Antony Cairns' oeuvre from his various cities/projects in London, Las Vegas, Tokyo and Osaka, (including LDN3, LDN4, LPT and OSC), interspersed with 6 texts by Simon Baker (senior curator of photography, Tate).'

- The artist's book-photobook: explore, experiment, interrogate, invent, personal, subjective, art

Jamais je ne T'oublierai (Bénitah 2019): 'I am rebuilding the memory of my family that I missed, I am inventing another one made to measure where I resurrect all the ancestors who have disappeared, the territories that I did not know and that have been praised to me.'

I Walk Toward the Sun which is Always Going Down (Huck 2019): 'In Alan Huck's image-text book, an unnamed narrator wanders a city in the American Southwest, where their observations and encounters become catalysts for rumination on a wide range of subjects. Shifting between photographs of the city's peripheries and an interior monologue written in first-person'.

- The photo essay-photobook: inform, document, research, witness, highlight, examine, reveal

American Origami (Gonzalez 2019): '*American Origami* is the result of six years of photographic research by Andres Gonzalez. The project closely examines the epidemic of mass shootings in American schools, interweaving first-person interviews, forensic documents, press materials, and original photographs.'

A Field Guide to Asbestos (Palu 2019): In *A Field Guide to Asbestos*, Louie Palu documents the effects of asbestos on people and the landscape in Canada, the US, India and the UK. In this 15-year-long award-winning investigative project, Palu also addresses the visual aspects of asbestos that are related to fatal diseases that can take up to 40 years after exposure before they appear.

There are of course hybrids, publications that operate in the in-betweens, and others where accompanying text may not underscore the message of the work, but it is worth remembering that one of the primary aims of identifying purpose-informed lineages is to underscore the intent in photographic publishing — something that is begun simply by holding these lineages up to published works. Lineages are not pivotal to other chapters in this book, but they certainly contribute to a more complete critical reckoning with the contemporary photobook. As part of this, I will place special significance on the photo essay-photobook — a lineage that is concerned most overtly with communication to a non-specialist public.[79] My argument regarding this lineage is predicated on a belief in the book as a valuable means of multi-sensory communication (see 'Photobooks & reading') that breaks through the omnipresence of digital content. As such, I propose that the photo essay-photobook has a particularly important role to play in engaging a readership beyond the photobook community.[80]

79
All lineages to an extent seek to communicate with a public, but in some, this communication is less urgent, and rooted less in the real-world experiences of readers as well as makers. For some works in the photo essay-photobook lineage, the makers have an ethical responsibility to the communities and subjects that they investigate.

80
There are, though, other perspectives on this matter that are worth acknowledging. Paul Soulellis suggests that a utopian vision of political artists' books encouraged by Lucy Lippard had come along, but not as expected. He proposes that digital message boards and downloadable content that are used to mobilise groups of protestors, are the contemporary iteration of the activist publication (Printed Matter 2021c). Similarly Lesley Martin imagines that we may have 'vacated' the territory of the photo essay-photobook and that Instagram and Snapchat are where the remit of this lineage is 'being most fulfilled'.

If what emerges from a reading of this chapter is a disagreement about categorisations, it will have provoked a fruitful interaction. But it is fair to say (with an emphasis on purpose so clearly raised here), that I intend to encourage more consideration of what it is that photobooks seek to do in the world and an honest[81] appraisal of makers' goals when putting ink to paper.

↳ Notes

As well as the taxonomies and spectrums introduced in this chapter (from Lesley Martin, Doug Spowart, Philip Zimmerman and Jörg Colberg), the doctoral work of José Luis Neves in *The Many Faces of the Photobook: Establishing the Origins of Photobookwork Practice* (2017) is well worth seeking out, as are the essays *Locating Photography and the Artist's Book* (2012) by Theresa Wilkie and Jane Pendlebury, *The Artist's Photographic Book: Towards a Definition* by Silvia Grace Borda (2012) (both handily found in the same publication) and Moritz Neumüller's *By the Book* (2017). Regarding the roots of the photobook, various names and publications are often brought up, with Kristen Lubben's *Partial Histories* (2019) tackling the contention of 'earliest photobook' privilege and Ian Walker's *A kind of 'Huh?': The Siting of Twentysix Gasoline Stations* (2012), as well as *Various Small Books* (Brouws et al. 2013) considering the influence of Ed Ruscha's works. Beyond the photobook, Michael Hampton's *Unshelfmarked* (2015) offers a view of alternative categorisations and a challenge to the canon of the artist's book.

81
The notion of honesty came up in two interviews — with Natasha Christia and Anshika Varma, both of whom cited this as a significant factor in the intention of publishing being realised.

Books to support the creation of lineages were presented in the main body text, but it is worth an accentuation of *Artists' Books: A Critical Anthology and Source Book* (Lyons 1985) which contains Alex

Sweetman's essay on the photobookwork, Ulises Carión's *The New Art of Making Books* and Lucy Lippard's The Artist's Book Goes Public. To engage with the breadth of intents in bringing work to a public, the collection *Publishing Manifestos* (Miss Read 2018) provides a wonderful beginning, which *Publishing as Artistic Practice* (Gilbert 2016) can flesh out, together with a consideration of an individual publishing practice like that found in Erik van der Weidje's *This is Not my Book* (2017). Alternative publishing and DIY approaches are well served in the likes of *Do or DIY* (Dworkin et al. 2012), *Anti-book: On the Art and Politics of Radical Publishing* (Thoburn, 2016) and *No ISBN: On Self-publishing* (Cella et al. 2015), as well as titles that can be easily found in relation to the underground press, radical publishing or zine culture (see Zinewiki for a rich resource here). Emily Larned's post *Publishing as (socially engaged) Artistic Practice* (2016) is insightful and borders on themes shared by activist publishing. One more to add is the conversation between Emma Bowkett, director of the *FT* weekend magazine and *Salvatore Vitale* (Vitale 2020), which looks at photographic stories reaching large audiences via the printed page in a progression of the principles of the photo essay.

I would suggest, though, that the most useful way in which to both decipher intent and consider the merits and failures of any taxonomic system is in personal application. In analysing the taxonomies and spectrums I encountered, and in the construction of my own, the books on my desk, those on my shelves and those in my institution's library were consistently encountered (so too was the virtual bookshelf of Josef Chladek,[82] the Photo-eye best-of lists and the canonical books on books from around the world). This exercise not only helped clarify my thinking, but revealed the many trends and intricacies that can be lost, and found, in categorisation. Perhaps these will help readers to witness, challenge or refine my own proposed lineages.

82 josefchladek.com

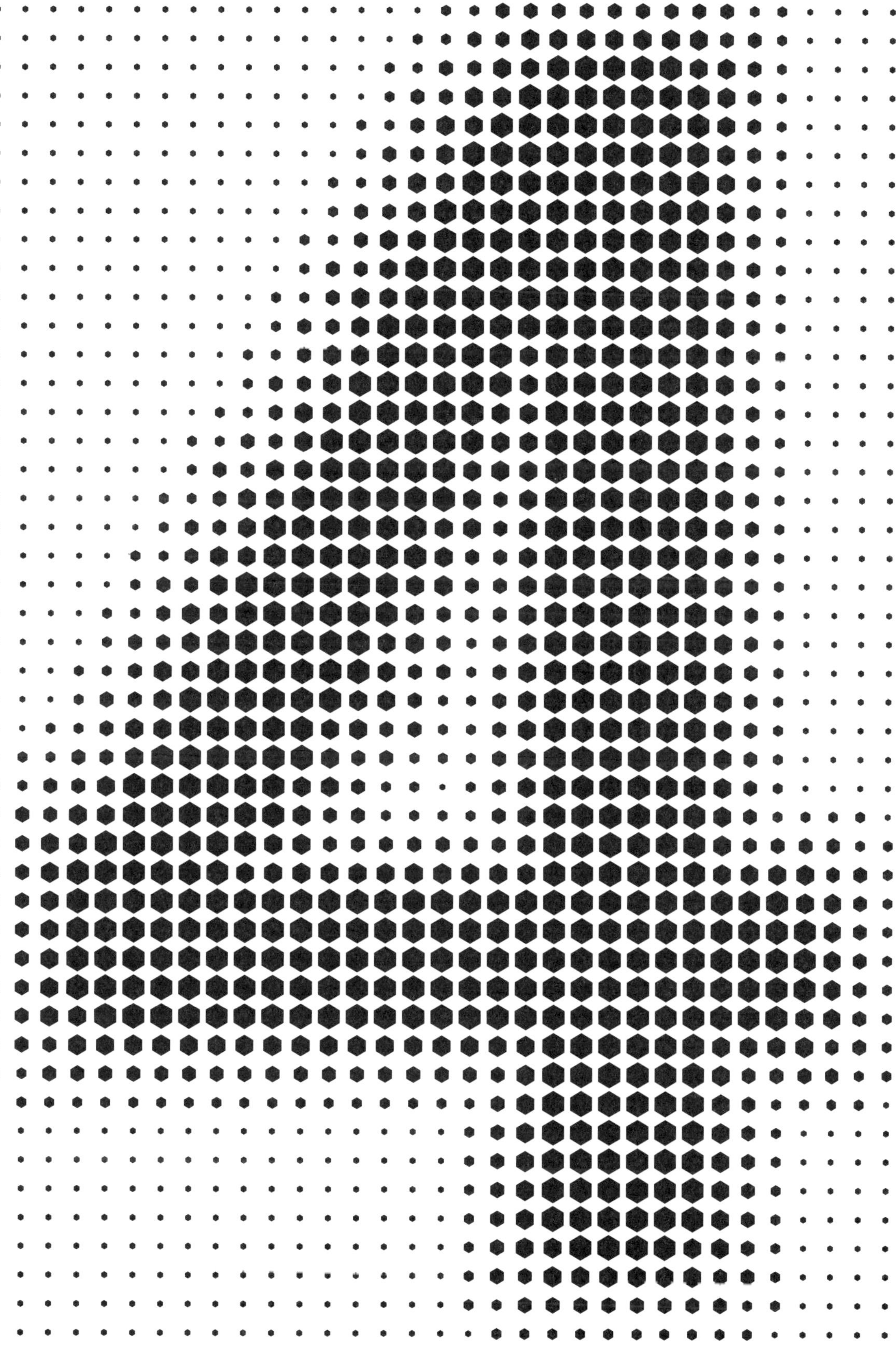

Photobooks & Access

With the portability of the book and the presence of dedicated photobook retailers, platforms and even libraries, it may seem strange to speak of the medium as having a restricted readership. But the contemporary photobook is poorly equipped to reach beyond the confines of the photobook community. To rectify this situation, we should look to ways in which the photobook can be augmented to engage audiences specific to the works themselves. Doing so will not only see our rich medium diversify, progress and prosper, but also contribute to constructive discourses about our world.

↳ The price of publishing

I have already proposed a correlation between the makeup and discourse of our photobook community as maker-centric, and the insularity of the medium ('Photobooks & community'). Here, I consider the effect this has on the form of publications themselves by addressing the content and construction of the contemporary photobook. I consider how the shape and even the subject matter of our contemporary medium can be understood as a product of our increasing concerns regarding production intricacies and quality, as well as an expanding interest in the minutiae and esotericism of intra-medium investigation.[83]

One of the crudest measurements to indicate a high-fidelity fascination and a maker-centric medium is also an important metric for the photobook's potential to reach new readers: cost. The average price of works that have been considered the best photobooks in the Photo-eye annual list over the past decade is consistently north of €30, with a vast amount of works above €50. The same is true if we look at shortlisted publications in Aperture's Photobook Award. There, of 10 titles for the award in 2020, the cheapest is €35.[84] The message that is constructed through awards and list-making like this may not be as extreme as a diktat that good books are expensive books, but at least that most good books are expensive.[85] And while for some, €30–50 is no great amount, if we think of an expanded audience, for whom the photobook is not a passion or artistic resource, it is hard to reconcile with any intention to use the photobook as a medium for communication beyond our small community. As Lesley Martin, publisher at Aperture clearly announces:

> 'When you talk about bigger audiences, then you do have to address two things. You have to address the form that you're creating and you

83
These trends can be attributed, at least in part, to the situation of the contemporary photobook in the post-millennium (see discussion in 'Photobooks & the post-digital'), but they are not exclusive to this moment. In an interview in 1978, A.D. Coleman spoke about the same issue: '[There's an] impulse to make the great book, not just in terms of imagery, or the coherence, but the reproduction has to be fantastic, and so on. It's wonderful; those books are lovely. But there are closets full of them all over America now' (Dugan 1979, 204).

84
It is not much different in the First Photobook Award, though three books hover around the €30-35 mark, and one is available (without shipping), for €22. Still, a greater number of books cost more than €50 than less.

85
I clearly make a subjective judgement here that €35 is expensive. I am supported by the fact that even those within the photobook community can be reluctant to spend €35 or so on a book (Alejandro Acin). This perspective is not universal, though. In speaking about their books, which retail around this figure, as part of the *Photobook Sessions* conference in 2021, Lewis Chaplin and Sarah Piegay Espenon of Loose Joints described them as both 'very affordable' and 'accessible to everyone' (2021). Such a view, I believe, is reflective of the insularity of the photobook community, which may well be the 'everyone' that is imagined.

have to address the price-point. And the two are obviously interrelated.'

It is true that making books is an expensive business, but financial requirements in production, which are then passed on to readers, are heightened in relation to post-millennium desires and maker- or production-centred discourse. Costs are often elevated via an increasing amount of 'unusual production flourishes' (Martin 2017):[86] multiple paper stocks, the use of fold-out pages, differently sized sheets and numerous binding types, which have helped separate the contemporary photobook from many of its historical predecessors. These choices have a direct impact on both haptic engagement and price. It is a challenging tension for the makers to balance the artistic possibilities of the book with cost repercussions, and it appears that it is the opportunities rather than resulting restrictions that have most often won out. Materiality has become a central feature of the medium, and has defined 'the specificity of a photobook as a (plat)form amongst other photographic spaces', creating a 'somewhat fetishistic sentiment within the photobook community' (Rose and Tuminas 2020, 195).

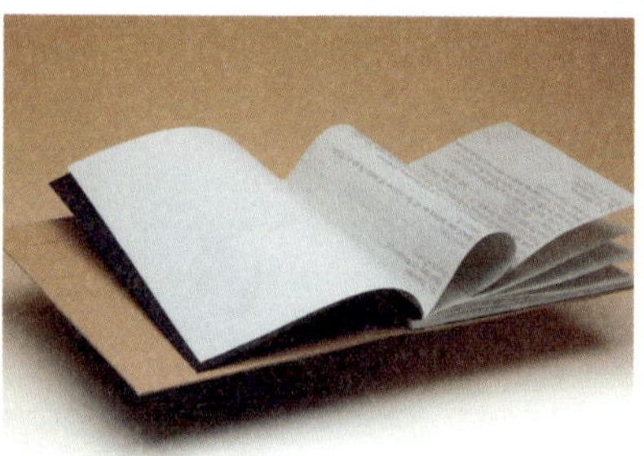

⊾ Cristina de Middel's *The Afroanuts* (2012), a hugely influential publication that embodies a new materiality of the photobook. Image courtesy of the artist.

Alongside the materiality of the photobook, our perception of, and desire for, quality must come into this discussion too. Michael Mack highlights how paper choice, printing and demands of the photographer for the utmost fidelity in reproduction[87] means that the 'result is something that ends up being very expensive' and that the 'fascination is then not with the original idea'. Mack's sentiment is a close companion to Florian Cramer's suggestion that in the post-digital, contemporary zines and other niche, experimental media are focusing 'less on content and more on pure materiality' (Cramer 2014), but there could be another influence. Bruno Ceschel notes how the decline of the small gallery may have contributed to the growth

86
Tiffany Jones' *Dynamics of the Photobook Market* gives us a perspective from the buyer. Of her 135 respondents to a survey on buying habits, 82% said that high-quality print and bind was either a must-have or preferred in a photobook they were deciding to buy. 59% looked for unique design and 53% for hardback, compared with only 21% for softcover (2019, 50).

87
In speaking about cinema, Hito Steyerl posits a fascination with 'pristine visuality' as a relation to 'systems of national culture, capitalist studio production, the cult of mostly male genius, and the original version' (2012, 35).

of the photobook. So, with the medium becoming significant in relation to a photographer's career (see 'Photobooks & the post-digital'), an emphasis on unique and high-end production qualities can be seen as an indicator that the photobook is partially filling the role of the gallery, with all the associated expectations regarding aesthetics and reproduction.

↳ Sophistication and exclusivity

Coupled with tensions between production and cost is the esotericism of the contemporary photobook — supported again by a discourse that often brings to the fore medium-specific considerations (whether photography, art or the photobook itself). As Larissa Leclair muses, 'I wonder whether some of the pieces that are created make sense to the general public'. With this in mind, a section from Ulises Carrión's text *The New Art of Making Books* from 1985 offers a parallel, sentiments of which are mirrored by the reflections of Colin Pantall and Alejandro Acin on the contemporary photobook:

> 'New art's language is radically different from daily language. It neglects intentions and utility, and it returns to itself, it investigates itself, looking for forms, for series of forms that give birth to, couple with, and fold into, space-time sequences' (Carrión 1985, 37–8).

> 'We contribute to the continuing introspective nature of photobooks ... They don't always address the world as it is, but rather introspect over the mechanics of how and why the photobook and its narratives operate' (Pantall 2012).

> 'Some photobooks are trying to communicate to a broader audience and some makers are only interested in the book being made ... There isn't always an interest in dissemination to a large audience.

> But then maybe some are making books to question the book itself and the book as a medium' (Alejandro Acin).

The introspection spoken of here pertains not only to the visual language of the photobook, but also to its subject matter. Perhaps in part as a reaction to the enormous shifts in life and image-making, photobooks often concern themselves with the workings of images in society. This is a worthwhile subject, but of limited interest to those who are not themselves involved in the field. Again, connections can be made with the artist's book, to Lucy Lippard's dashed hopes for the democratic nature of the medium, which became 'avant-garde art' (Ault 2006), and to Clive Philpot's suggestion that few books connect with everyday issues or concerns beyond the arts community (2012, 136). Lately, the situation is being noticed in regards to the contemporary photobook,[88] with Dolly Meieran of 10x10 Photobooks citing the need for 'responsibility among bookmakers' to produce works that have value outside the maker's own practice. A dedicated photobook community, comprised of other makers, however, helps maintain and extend esoteric publications, for there is a niche audience who will understand and engage with such works. Thus, it takes considerable effort[89] to expose ourselves to the fluctuations and uncertainty of a readership beyond.

The result of all this is an increasingly refined and cultivated form of the photobook that may well be witnessed by those inside the photobook community casting a glance over their bookshelves or making comparisons with pre-millennium works. The luxury of shared reference points, frequent meetings and medium-dedicated resources in the form of events, digital platforms and a myriad of photobook-making workshops all provide valuable fuel for the growth not only of the medium in scale but in literacy too. This is a product of what Lesley Martin has called a 'spiralling sophistication':[90]

88
This debate is not exclusive to contemporary photobooks. Ivan Vartanian speaks about how many Japanese works in the 1960s and 70s could 'only be understood by people "in the know"' and that beyond an audience that was very close to the maker, much of it will have appeared 'opaque' (2009, 12).

89
At the *Photobook Sessions* conference in 2021, David Solo mused as to whether reviews and critical writing on photobooks should seek to contextualise references, histories or symbolism on which some photobooks rely.

90
In speaking with photographer Amani Willett, he too sees this spiral of sophistication and offers a reminder that it is taking place 'in a vacuum' within the 'community of bookmakers and artists and photographers', thus widening a gap with a broader readership.

‘The [photobook] form that gives photographers the greatest measure of creative freedom and precision is also a form that’s so expensive to produce, so difficult to support and publicise at the level of mainstream culture, thus so expensive to sell, and thus in such short supply.’ (Wolukau-Wanambwa 2019)

Fig. 9

The spiralling sophistication of
the contemporary photobook

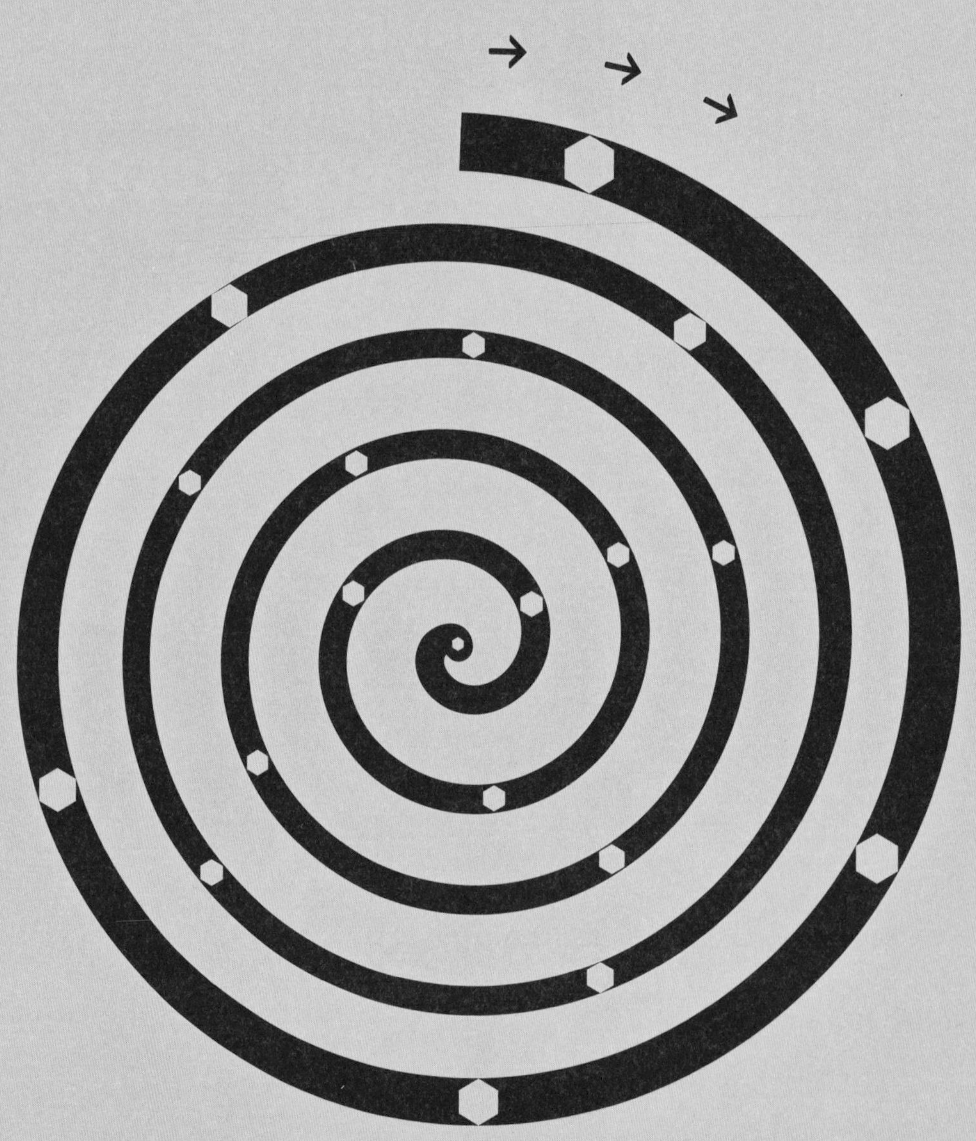

> 'You get into a spiral of increasingly more and more arcane projects, which is one of the things that I think is a potential downside and danger of the increasingly insular world of the photobook ... We're becoming more limited in who we're speaking to, because there's certainly a fall off, I think, in people who have the time to commit to learning how to read the photobook.'

This trajectory for the photobook may not be surprising, given the community, discourse and post-digital location charted in the pages of *Photobooks &*, but it is a notable adjustment that has occurred in a short space of time. In 2004, Gerry Badger and Martin Parr positioned the medium between the esoteric and the everyday: Badger referred to it as coming 'somewhere between the mass medium and the hermetic art form' (2004, 10) and that as such it is a 'vital interstice ... between the journeyman and the artist, between the aesthetic and the contextual' (2004, 11). I would argue that the occupation of a middle ground on this spectrum has not been retained. The rising sophistication of the visual and material production of photobooks, combined with a discourse that emphasises these very qualities, engenders a new sort of insularity that impacts the potential of the photobook to reach beyond its limited enclave.

Though the photobook community may not be fully conscious of this insularity, there is an undercurrent in intra-medium communication that revels in esotericism and works that overtly counter the mainstream.[91] Trolley Books' Hannah Watson notes that photographers want 'the small and interesting books that aren't mass market commercial things' (Smyth et al., 2015, 27)[92] and Lesley Martin suggests that thinking of a broader audience for the photobook may be restricted because there is an assumption that doing so might be perceived as 'pandering'. This perception is representative of an interesting strain between the specialist

91
An article I wrote about the counter-commercial materiality of the photobook for *Over Journal* will be published in late 2021.

92
A situation mirrored in some artists' books, where 'the aesthetic and conceptual underpinnings' of the medium 'stem partially from a reaction against mass production and commercialisation' and where an ease of access 'could be seen as opposing the movement's principles, where artists typically share work at book fairs, via mail order, or through independent bookshops' (Verity 2012, 93–4).

and the mass-market demonstrated by the lack of works intended for large audiences in photobook discourse, lists and competitions. What the spiral of sophistication and insular community of the photobook construct, then, is a situation whereby efforts to reach broader audiences via small adjustments or augmentations are seen as challenges to the privilege, integrity and artistic freedom of the makers.[93]

↳ The inert photobook

What compounds some of the rifts we face in access and readership due to the contemporary photobook's sophistication and insularity is a belief in the book as an inherently active medium. Conversations regarding the merit of the printed page over the gallery or museum wall are frequent in the photobook community, and rely on an assumption that the medium is one of democratic mobility. The belief may be best summed up in El Lissitzky's remark that:

> 'In contrast to the old monumental art [the book] itself goes to the people, and does not stand like a cathedral in one place waiting for someone to approach' (Lissitzky in Ludovico 2012, 35).

This is a fallacy born of the photobook's potential for mobility, which is in fact often overridden by its default and inherent inertia.[94] I would argue that the book is, without action, a medium of chance encounters at best. Its great and immeasurable possibilities and opportunities come only as a result of significant and wilful action of makers and a network of individuals involved in distribution and dissemination. This action is what Michael Bhaskar would call *amplification*[95] — the act of increasing the readership of a given work (2013, 114). Amplification, as Bhaskar formulates it, is primarily about increasing circulation, but I would like to add for the purpose of discussing access to

93
The freedom that has emerged from the separation of the artistic mind and intent from the rigidity of maker-reader relationships and traditional market influences brings to mind Lucy Lippard's comment that perhaps artists' books are a 'state of mind' (Lippard 1985, 56).

94
Lesley Martin: 'If you want to have a dialogue you can't just put a book out into the world and expect it's going to make an impact. You actually do have to extend the reach of that book.'

95
Bhaskar's term 'amplification' fits within his theory of publishing that begins with the decision to make a work public (filtering), before developing a suitable platform for the work (framing), and then seeking to disseminate and publicise (amplification). Found in *The Content Machine* (2014), Bhaskar's theory may be of considerable help to some makers embarking on a publishing project.

photobooks, the term *activation*. Activation describes an energising of the book through invitations, events, workshops and even republishing — strategies that generate a readership rather than only an increased audience.[96] This addition places significantly more responsibility on the maker to not only get their photobook into the hands of intended readers, but to create space for, or facilitate, the reading itself.

Thought regarding amplification and activation provides a counter to Natasha Christia's accusation (employing Boris Groys' term) that the photobook is a 'defunctionalised cultural artefact' (2020). Christia justifies this criticism in terms of the ways in which we have constructed a history, set of terms, collection of authoritative voices and market values in the space of two decades that venerate and ritualise the photobook.[97] Challenging this, she proposes, will require new reflections on existing and imminent works, in particular, shifting our perception and treatment of the photobook as a final and completed work that marks the end of a project, to a point in a chronology of communication.

Rather than amplification and activation in the form of 'people talking about their work in front of other people' as happens in the photobook community, makers could look 'for more active ways to engage people' (Natasha Christia). This is uncomfortable for many, as illustrated in Christia's reflections on a workshop in which participants who had brought books-in-progress along were asked to exchange with another practitioner who could then make interventions in the work, an act 'met with much resistance' (2020).[98] However, this example illustrates the need to unsettle our established ways of thinking about publishing, which have become formulaic and restricted.

Publishing, then, must be considered as a series of acts that both extend the reach of a given work (amplification) and provide assistance for engagement with

96
The distinction here is that activation must construct a conducive environment for reading rather than assume that the book's arrival in the hands of a reader is necessarily enough. This may simply be a space, or it may be an introduction or framing of particular books to provide an opening for the reader (much like The Photobook Club's online and in-person readings).

97
There are parallels here with photography's location in Pierre Bourdieu's spheres of legitimisation: 'Faced with meaning situated outside the sphere of legitimate culture, consumers feel they have the right to remain pure consumers and judge freely; on the other hand, within the field of consecrated culture, they feel measured according to objective norms, and forced to adopt a dedicated, ceremonial and ritualised attitude' (Bourdieu 1996, 95).

98
'The radical de-familiarisation from their "own" object that took place in front of their eyes put participants in a vulnerable position, bringing to the fore the community's aversion toward experimentation. Everybody expected an outcome until everyone realised that the outcome went beyond the production of visual artefacts. It was the very *situation* of resistance and its negotiation in public that mattered' (Christia 2020).

it (activation). So while innovative promotional strategies and distribution tactics are an integral part, they do not provide a holistic response to the issues of the venerated and insular photobook. This is an important distinction when we acknowledge the sophistication and self-referential nature of the photobook, which can install barriers for new readers.

Where the responsibility for this re-awakening of the photobook's potentiality falls is a topic for debate (see 'Photobooks & the future'), though Christia proposes that the financial and logistical obligation of publishers means that it should lie primarily with the practitioners.[99]

↳ Acts of amplification and activation

There is no blueprint for a re-functionalising of the photobook, since makers must honestly assess the intentions of the publication of the work (see 'Photobooks & intent' as well as the questions featured in 'Photobooks & the future'). I shall, though, present a few interesting case studies that may pose points of inquiry for the reader about the ongoing interplay between intent, form, access and audience. These short studies are not chosen so as to evidence all possible acts of amplification or activation, but to show how some practitioners have reflected on their intent in publishing and responded with deliberate choices in making work public. To begin, Mathieu Asselin's *Monsanto: A Photographic Investigation* published by Kettler Verlag in 2017, has much to offer this discussion.

Asselin's photographic investigation explores the murky world of the agrochemical giant Monsanto and its impact on lives and land in the US and abroad (placing this work firmly in the lineage of the photo essay-photobook outlined in 'Photobooks & intent'). It combines Monsanto's own advertising with newspaper clippings,

99
Already there are publishers who take the communicating of a message beyond the art and photography audience as their responsibility. Perhaps there is space for more of this, and for publishers to gain a reputation for their innovative and efficient acts of 'making public' alongside their prestige in the photobook ecology and quality of reproductions and material.

‘What becomes obvious is that conceiving the (photo)book as an encounter and an event automatically raises demands on us and on what we can do with it. We are in need of generating more creative ‘situations’ when it comes to engaging with books. Situations that re-orchestrate the moment of writing and reading, and allow for more inclusive environments of hospitality, discussion and knowledge production touching upon all categories of society.’ (Christia 2020)

Fig. 10

10.1 The containment of the photobook ecology

10.2 The need for amplification and activation

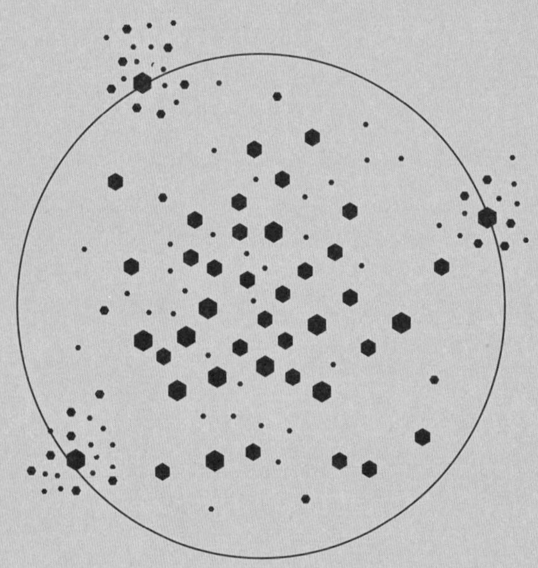

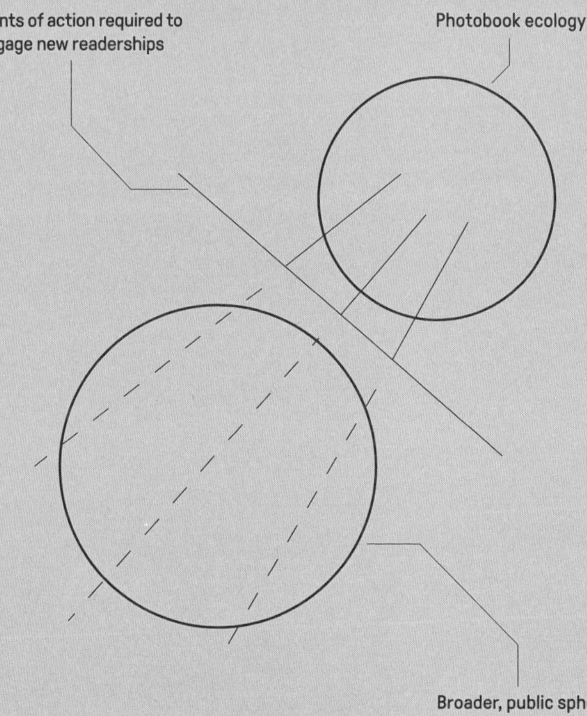

video stills, essays, maps and Asselin's photographs. It is comprehensive, clearly the result of significant time in research and production, and is literally and figuratively a heavyweight book. It's imposing stature suggests the rigour, seriousness and authoritative nature of the project, but can also be said to restrict certain avenues of amplification and activation.[100]

By way of response, and thinking of the work in a rhizomatic fashion, Asselin has sought ways for the work to spark conversation via exhibitions at The Photographers Gallery, London, FotoMuseum Antwerp and crucially (in engaging a political sphere of conversation), the European Parliament building in Strasburg, all accompanied by free newspapers featuring a condensed version of the book within. With such activities, Asselin has gone some way to amplifying the work in order to reach broader audiences, though even these are relatively exclusive spaces. It is an intricate relationship, balancing aspirations in the art and photobook ecology as well as desires to speak to a public beyond and one that is impacted by subject matter and intent of publishing.[101] Alejandro Acin points out that Asselin's photobook is only one part of a bigger strategy, and Asselin himself recognises that success in his career helps more works to emerge, and for them to carry an increasing audience. Still, he is frank when discussing the limits of the original publication. He speaks of the need for a cheaper, smaller second edition, and has also combated some of the limits of the initial publication in releasing a digital iteration, made available for free with a fair-use licence.

> 'It's a simple as: many people didn't have access to the book for different reasons, one being the price, so the idea is to make it accessible to everyone with an internet connection. In a few weeks, more people have download the book than the total English sales of the book – people from everywhere. That's a wonderful thing' (Mathieu Asselin).

100
When I questioned Asselin on the expense of the book he acknowledged that 'it was not very democratic even in the EU' but that it was 'important to have a book like that ... and the book as an object'. His subsequent actions have greatly assisted in creating a more democratic approach to publishing than most other works with a similar cost.

101
In an echo of the successful work that Asselin undertook with various media outlets, the publisher (Tiffany Jones) and photographer (Amani Willett) of *A Parallel Road* (2020) spoke of some significant moments of breakthrough to a broader audience as a result of engagement with mainstream press — the *Boston Globe*, NPR and PBS. While presence in outlets of this scale may not always be attainable, many local and regional platforms carry considerable audiences of engaged readers (certainly so in comparison with photobook-specific outlets).

Very different from Asselin in terms of the intent of her publishing activities, Dyanita Singh is an interesting practitioner to consider in relation to amplification. While her publications may not always seek readership beyond the art world, she embraces vastly different models of publishing for each piece of work – a reactive and project-driven approach to making public.[102] Of particular note here is *Chairs* (2005),[103] a work constructed as a mini exhibition with an accordion-folded set of 22 images in a limited-edition publication. While the print run of only 500 and the visual language and subject matter of *Chairs* may not offer the most democratic of publishing examples, it perfectly reveals the possibility of bespoke distribution. By giving a set of 10 copies to 50 individuals to pass on without cost, Singh subverts the traditional market-oriented network and engages the mobility of the book. In enlisting different hubs of circulation in the form of autonomous humans, she also calls upon a sentient model of dissemination that morphs into a reflection on its unique contexts. In speaking about the project, Singh recounts how some distributors would select particular individuals to receive a copy, while others would see this as elitist and give them to the first people they saw that day — the bus driver, receptionist and so on (Printed Matter 2021a). Thus, the book remains within a community of enthusiasts and extends beyond it.[104]

I have undertaken some work in amplifying and activating the photobook myself. In 2011, Ken Schles' *Invisible City* (1988), a book about New York's East Village in the 1980s, was read on The Photobook Club.[105] Following a month-long look at the work online, and with contributions from a range of readers, I set about augmenting the conversation in an ebook and interactive PDF. The content provided a considered, contextual account of the original book and, with Schles' commitment to facilitating greater access, I was able to include his insights into the production

102
'The work never stops for me when the book is made. It's just the start of phase two and phase three ... you must find ways to activate it ... whether it is through a simple discussion or thinking of innovative ways to take the book to the people' (Dyanita Singh, in Printed Matter 2021a).

103
It is also worth noting Singh's *Zakir Hussain Maquette* (2019), in which her earlier photobook *Zakir Hussain* (1986), a rare and out-of-print work, is returned to and situated anew with a publication that not only features a replication of the original dummy (or maquette) that Singh made, but a new fold-out poster and reader companion all enclosed within the slipcase. The reader helps to contextualise the original publication and revitalise it for a new audience.

104
This model may still privilege the expert or revered critic: Singh tells of a meeting with artist Sol LeWitt in which she learned he had already been gifted three copies (Printed Matter 2021a).

105
Chosen for its iconic status and lack of availability, *Invisible City* was a perfect publication to open up to a new audience. What was particularly fortuitous here was that Schles, as the work's author, was himself frustrated by the limits of access to the book, which (with a secondhand value around $1,000) meant that, with few exceptions, the book was retained within a small community of designers, photographers and book collectors.

and life of *Invisible City*. Alongside his original lecture notes from a talk at the International Centre of Photography in New York, and his musings on the cult status of the work, was a video of an alternative edit of Invisible City, one that Schles called *Night Walk* (since published by Steidl). The resulting publication was titled *Invisible City: A digital Resource,* and within the first six months had been downloaded more than 2,000 times,[106] a significant figure that matched the original print run for *Invisible City*. Schles speaks about the project in a section of Darius Himes and Mary Virginia Swanson's *Publish your Photography Book*, articulating his frustration about how many great photobooks remain 'hidden', and asking 'what would our world be if science were so obscured?' (2014, 148).

This act of amplification and activation is only of a single publication, but it demonstrates not only how augmentation and republication can vastly increase readership, but also that such acts do not adversely impact the demand for the paid-for, physical publication. Thus, the maker is not fiscally disadvantaged with the increase in awareness of and access to the publication via digital means.[107] In Schles' own words:

> 'The digital experience neither replicates nor replaces an experience of a physical book. But then it isn't meant to. It stands on its own merits...what was once a dead end now lives within the context of a dynamic and engaged conversation ... you are welcome to savour this eBook study before committing to the rare copy...or the beautiful reprint from Steidl — for free' (Himes and Swanson, 2014, 149).[108]

↳ The role of the library, collection and exhibition

Perhaps the most significant acts of amplification and activation of the contemporary photobook have not

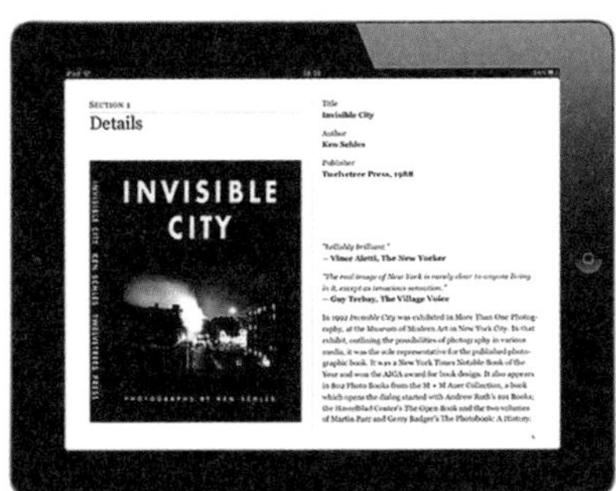

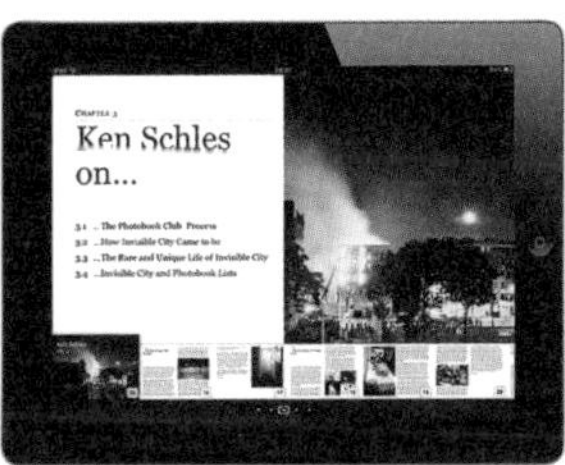

↳ *Invisible City: A Digital Resource* (2012). Image is author's own.

106
It was well received, featuring in *European Photography* as one of Markus Schaden's picks of the best digital photobooks (Schaden 2013, 71) and described by writer Taco Hidde Bakker as one of 'the most surprising 2012 photobook publications', which he reflects upon as 'an excellent example of how ... photobooks can be lifted out of the shadows and be studied in a public realm beyond the traditional library' (Bakker 2012).

107
When the photobook community is the primary consumer of the photobook, and its makers (and thus readers) seek out the haptic experience of the book, what harm is there in experimenting with lower-fidelity works, accompanying digital offerings and cheaper reprints?

108
Invisible City was republished by Steidl in 2014 and it had a second printing in 2016.

involved (or been led by) makers, but individuals and organisations who have championed the medium and constructed libraries, archives, reading rooms and workshops to engage the photobook community, and a broader public.[109] These platforms adopt a variety of approaches to their unique remits, but common threads are found in the photobook's presence in spaces that do not impose barriers or restrictions to entry or access,[110] and an acknowledgement of the need for action to increase engagement and support reading.[111]

The physical positioning of the photobook is significant in generating readership. If it is found only in photobook fairs, galleries or contemporary art museums, it will already be restricted in its potential. Likewise, archives and collections that are out-of-the-way will have to work harder to encounter those not seeking out the experience they offer. This is something that Ángel González of The Library Project, which is based in a tourist spot (Temple Bar, Dublin), has been thinking about. González acknowledges that while there are challenges in terms of space with the current location, it presents significant opportunities, with people passing by from all over the world, and that to move to larger premises away from the centre of the city would alter the footfall and makeup of the audience.[112]

For some initiatives, it is their travelling components — in the form of temporary exhibitions and reading rooms — that provide opportunities to move out of an established art environment. Russet Lederman of 10x10 Photobooks extolled the value of having a reading room in the New York Public Library because it allowed for engagement beyond an art audience — to tourists and 'people who know nothing about photobooks' walking into a space that has a mandate to interact with the public free of charge. But finding a location for the photobook is only a single aspect of the work that these projects undertake. Anshika Varma of Offset Projects speaks about the need for invitation,

109
Examples include the Indie Photobook Library (now closed), 10x10 Photobooks, Offset Projects, Reminders Photography Stronghold, The Asia-Pacific Photobook Archive, Hydra, The Photobook Museum, The Library Project, Africa in the Photobook, the Mobile Library of the Asia Art Archive and my own Photobook Club.

110
Galleries, museums and specialist art locations are to many, exclusive spaces, engagement with which requires particular knowledge or training. This is gradually shifting with changing mandates and emerging public-art platforms, but the perception is still significant.

111
I would propose that while these initiatives are hugely beneficial, and would be, regardless of the situation makers constructed, their need and introduction is a reflection of the exclusivity of the photobook medium and a missing link between makers and readers. Where responsibility for access lies is discussed further in 'Photobooks & the future'.

‘One thing that I really imbibed from photojournalism: the importance of the dissemination of the image. And if I can’t do anything else, if no one wanted to show or publish my work, I could project my images from this hotel room onto those clouds and put my work out there. There is always a way, once you step out of the box that photography often can be.’ (Dyanita Singh in Martin 2018)

‘The education team was met with spontaneous interest every day from people willing to take a moment of time for photobooks. Whether they came with rollerblades on their feet, their dog on a leash, a bike, or a pram, visitors could bring whatever they had with them into the exhibition space. That made it easier for people to enter the experience.’ (Bicher 2020, 160)

and a carefully considered environment to facilitate reading.[113] By including small texts beside each book on uncluttered tables, her reading rooms seek to construct a situation for an uninterrupted reading in which anyone 'can have a relationship with a book with nothing else there; there is nothing in the middle':

> 'How you organise the space in which you place the book becomes very very important ... I make sure that there's always a chair that invites you to sit with each book. It's a small thing, but to know that [you] can sit down and look at the book completely changes engagement' (Anshika Varma).

For a very thorough account of a conscious effort to challenge the exclusivity of the medium and see it thrive in a broader readership, we could turn to the mobile photobook project *A World in Transition*, a collaboration between the Photobook Museum and the Montag Stiftung Kunst und Gesellschaft. The project saw a travelling exhibition of photobooks placed in high-footfall public spaces: public squares in Rostock, Duisburg and Kassel. But this alone was recognised only as a necessary foundation, so on top of the exhibition, the team developed an outdoor installation of photographs, a catalogue workshop,[114] a café and a series of photobook sessions that enabled people with no prior knowledge of the medium to produce a photobook dummy. Clearly, the *World in Transition*[115] project was very well-funded — with a team of individuals, significant logistical support and partners in the city itself. But this is not to say that the model cannot be wielded by others on a smaller scale. Barrier-less entry, social spaces for conversation and workshops do not have to involve containers positioned in city centres, but could instead be in local cafés, community centres, schools and even retail environments.

What these vignettes of different approaches to amplification and/or activation show is just a few ways in

112 ⮐
Bricks and mortar location and its impact on a medium is not new to the field of artists' books. Clive Philpot spoke of the significance of Printed Matter moving from Tribeca to Soho in the 1980s and Bruno Ceschel cites the New York Art Book Fair's move from Chelsea to PS1 in 2011 as coinciding with a massive expansion of the event and medium (2019). We could also look at Ami Clarke's Banner Repeater at Hackney Downs railway station as a great example of situating the book (artist's book in this project's case) in a high-traffic, democratic location.

113
Echoing the need for thought beyond availability alone, Susanna Chung, who runs the Mobile Library of the Asia Art Archive, describes the library as a catalyst for new possibilities in which it is public programming that helps to activate the works once access is established (Offset Projects 2020).

114
Visitors were able to 'compile their own exhibition catalogue free of charge' (Bicher 2020, 157).

115
The project is written about in detail (including lessons learned from elements that were less successful) in The Photobook in Art and Society (2020).

which the photobook can break away from the confines of our community whilst also retaining a place inside.[116] Multiple editions (*Monsanto*), innovative distribution (*Chairs*), contextual republishing (*Invisible City*), curated spaces and strategic outreach (10x10 Photobooks, The Library Project, Offset Projects and *World in Transition* et al.), may offer some points of departure or conversation for makers who can find specific questions to ask of their practice in the culmination of this publication: 'Photobooks & the future'.

↳ Notes

To begin, I'll point out a few different publications or practitioners with amplification and/or activation acts that may provide thoughts for the reader that I did not list in the main text. Alongside Mark Neville and Susan Meiselas, who are both well known for seeking to engage the community (and landscape) of their works post-publication, we might also look at Ethan Rafal's *Shock and Awe* (2015) book tour, the events that accompanied Harrell Fletcher's publication *The American War* (2006) and Dutch publishing house Paradox. Each project on which Paradox works (with a documentary specialism) is realised across a spectrum of outputs that might include school activities, digital publications, exhibitions and interactive websites.

There are participatory publishing events to consider — like Daido Moriyama's printing show (Tate, 2012),[117] Takeshi Homma's *RRREECCONNSTRUCCTTT* (2014), Jean Wainwright's *Border Line: Rights of Passage* (2015) and *On Hold* by Richard Higginbottom and Jack Greenwood (2018), as well as the less active, but no less significant gestures of makers like Max Pinkers, who has made his sold-out books available for free as

116
There will of course be publications for which such amplification and activation is not desired. If makers truly intend only to speak with the photobook community, little activation is required, since the audience is primed for engaging with the form, and even amplification can be simplified to a set of acts that might include: sending copies to reviewers, tastemakers and list-constructors; getting the book sold in key sites and shops; producing a signed, limited edition with print and engaging with interviews or talks with photography and photobook-specific platforms.

117
First performed in 1974, it was at Aperture Gallery in 2011 and at Tate Modern in 2012.

PDF downloads. The approach to publishing and access of science-fiction writer and journalist Cory Doctorow is a fascinating case study that is complemented by a photographic collaboration with Jonathan Worth (Foto8 2010). Book launches and photobook conversations that have tended to be held in galleries, bookshops and other physical spaces have, since the COVID-19 pandemic, often relocated online. The benefit for the researcher is significant. Outputs from Offest Projects (*the guftgu series*), MACK (MACK LIVE) and 10x10 Photobooks (#INSTAsalons) all offer insights into how books have come about, their intentions, and amplification and activation tactics (which if nothing else includes the events themselves).

My own Photobook Club, and moreover the incredible communities that really propel the initiative, have introduced and run a great variety of projects that have sought to amplify and activate the photobook. Added to the meetings themselves, which operate in a relaxed and inclusive manner, is World Photobook Day, where readers are encouraged to share thoughts, donate books and ask friends or neighbours over, and there have been workshops, talks, reading rooms and the wonderful *book jockey* events founded by Bonifacio Bario Hijosa. The main website (photobookclub.org) is a good place to get a sense of the project, and from there, the events page links to the various communities around the globe.

The texts I found most helpful in my research into access and the photobook were undoubtedly Simon Bhaskar's *The Content Machine* (2014) and Natasha Christia's *The (photo)book: On Potentiality*, the latter of which was only published in 2020 but was so instrumental that I quickly set up a conversation with Christia. There is much from Bhaskar's work that I haven't included here — his speaking about 'frames' and publishing 'models' in particular. I have borrowed those terms in other writing and would encourage engagement with this text, which can offer a great deal to those grappling with the messiness of publishing (from a maker's or scholar's perspective).

Lucy Lippard's writing on the artist's book in public spaces is also worth seeking out, as is Simon Cutt's *Some Forms of Availability* (2007), Clive Phillpot's 1978 essay *Some Questions about Book Art* (2013) and of course the extensive reflections on the photobook engaging with broader audiences in *The photobook in Art and Society: Participative Potentials of a Medium* (The Photobook Museum & Montag Stiftung Kunst und Gesellschaft 2020). Finally, Anshika Varma's guftgu conversation with Susanna Chung (Offset Projects 2020) gives a considerable amount to think about in terms of the role and actions of libraries to engage with a readership.

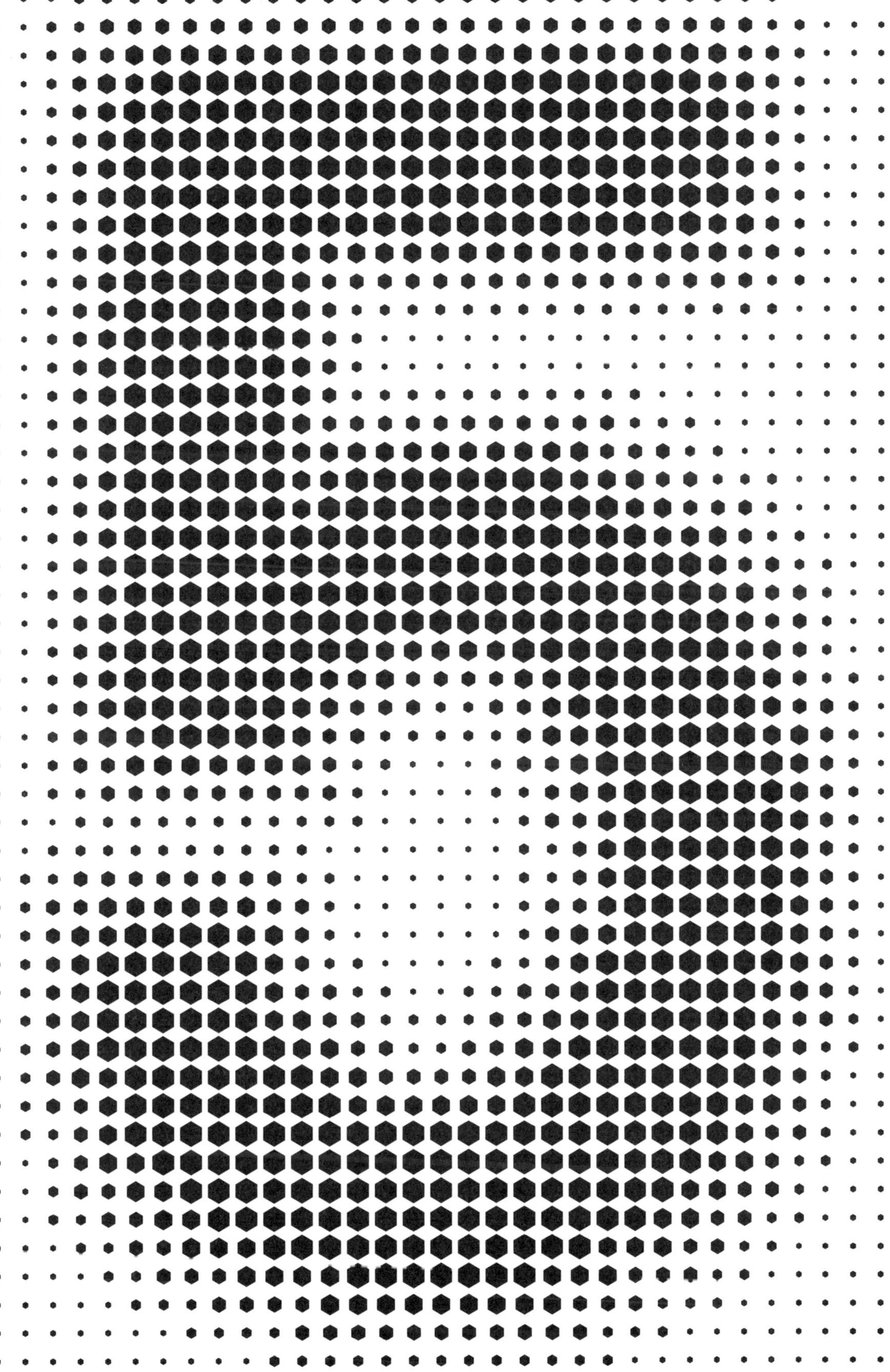

Photobooks & Reading

The reader is an overlooked individual in the ecology of the photobook. A product of the omnipresent maker and maker-centric discourse, this is also a result of the difficulty we have in speaking about our experience with photobooks. How can we account for reading when it is unique to each of us, and engages so many faculties and performances? Spanning the visual, literary and material, photobook reading is complex, but grappling with it is a worthwhile endeavour. In documenting reading, and in providing a structure and language for the subject, the reader is harder to neglect, and the achievement of a more balanced publishing landscape becomes possible.

↳ What do we do when we read a photobook?

> 'A book is a real thing we can touch, feel, and enact by turning pages. Our own thoughts get infused with new ideas as we page through the book, binding images and texts to one another and to our own mental images and sensations' (Tate Shaw 2016, 140).

With all the attention directed towards the contemporary photobook over the last two decades, little has been spared for the reader, or the act of reading.[118] Where conscious reflections on the subject of reading do occur, they tend to be highly personal in nature. Certainly an important component in making the reader more visible, these insights are minimal in comparison to the impression of photobook reading we get in the form of the review, or feature article. Rather than contributing to an understanding of how reading the photobook is conducted or experienced, these texts often defunctionalise[119] the work at hand and adopt an attitude of reverence and celebration. This can be attributed in part to maker-centrism (see 'Photobooks & community'), and a discourse that is often focused on aesthetics and materiality, but may also be accounted for in the difficulty of speaking about a hybrid medium that brings together multiple sensorial elements, and which is realised only through the wilful engagement and thought of an individual reader.

By way of response, I have sought to provide a research-led account of photobook reading that articulates and evidences the significant role of the reader in encounters with the photobook. It is proposed that in shifting attention from the esoteric choices of the makers, to the role and understanding of the reader, we may open a connection between the two that is otherwise absent or vastly abstracted.

118
There are a few spaces in which attempts to translate or describe the experience of reading the photobook have taken place, which are introduced later in this chapter.

119
A term used by Natasha Christia and expanded on in 'Photobooks & access'. Christia speaks of the recently constructed histories, terms, authoritative voices and market values of the photobook as contributors to the veneration and ritualisation of the medium.

Developing an account of photobook reading is far from straightforward. The complexity of the medium as one that intersects various visual and textual fields of theory demands a catered approach to research. For my process, this has meant a 'plugging in' of data with literature in a way that has sought to 'open up and proliferate' rather than 'foreclose' knowledge (Jackson and Mazzei 2011, vii). It has meant the combining of extensive data collected from a survey of 187 photobook readers, graphical elicitation of reading habits[120] with 27 individuals, and engagement with texts and theory from across the arts, cinema, photography, materiality and literature. In order to provide some structure and clarity to what is a melée of sources and avenues of investigation, presented in this chapter are some of the most significant findings from the research, structured around four key aspects of engaging with the photobook: handling the photobook as an object; looking at the photobook as a montage; reading the photobook as a text; and constructing a unique reading. Ultimately, the coming together of established theories and up-to-date photobook-specific reflections in these pages lead to the formation of eight acts of photobook reading[121] designed as a common space for conversation between makers and readers.

↳ Handling the photobook as an object

Materiality is a key aspect of our engagement with the photobook, but existing ruminations on the subject with a focus on reading (rather than production) are few.[122] Whilst the physical form of the photobook from a taxonomic or production perspective features in the pages of many publications seeking to offer overviews of the medium, it is not often that the impact of haptics on the reading experience is recognised. One supportive work from the adjacent field of the artist's book[123] is found in Tim Daly's *Book Handling as a Research Method* (2018). Daly stresses that

120
Graphical elicitation is a method of data collection and subsequent analysis that can be used to assist the review of experience and emotion, complementing 'data collected through the interviewing process' and 'stimulating thoughts' (Copeland and Agosta 2012, 514).

121
These acts are designed as a malleable and useable account that does not describe or impose what a reading should be, but offers a common ground for discourse.

122
Yumi Goto and the Reminders Photography Stronghold, for example, emphasise the materiality of the photobook in their *Photobook as object* workshops, but these concentrate on the construction rather than reception of the book.

123
As noted in the introduction, the relationship between photobooks and artists' books is not the subject of this publication. Nevertheless, much can be understood from the more extensive research that has been conducted into these visual, codex-based works, which share many attributes with the contemporary photobook. For example, attention to the objecthood of the artist's book has been ongoing for some time, with many of Clive Phillpot's essays in *Booktrek* (2012) offering a good introduction to the discourse.

ignoring the handling of a work would be to miss out on 'entire swathes of intertextual nuances ... the deliberate choices of the artist' (2018). Daly announces touch as a 'fundamental aspect of interacting with books', which are designed and destined to be handled at 'close-quarters', far away from the formality and distance imposed by artwork on walls of galleries and museums (2018). Though this call for consideration of handling accentuates the form of the book as art-object, Daly's approach also highlights how the unique material experience of the book as a medium that is operated by the hand, eye and mind enriches its communicative potential.[124]

Whether a product of our post-digital and post-photographic desires and preferences, or established in our relationship with books more broadly, survey responses regarding reading often begin with a considerable discussion of the book's physical properties. What is interesting in the responses is the frequent presence of a separation between the physical and otherwise — 'first' is the physical examination and 'then' is the 'beginning' of reading. This is not to say that the physical is subsequently ignored, but that it is not as overtly present as at the very first interaction with the work. This may be an innate occurrence for the book, which must be handled before it can be operated, or read.

> 'The first thing I do is feel the material — the heft of the book, the cloth, the paper ... the form of the object informs the content. Then I start at the beginning.'[125]

> 'First I examine its physical construction, the cover, the binding, the paper stock, the printing. Then I examine how it begins.'

Even a little time spent at a photobook fair, or reading reviews, blurbs or interviews pertaining to specific photobooks, shows that the physicality of the

124
Multi-sensory learning theory purports that: 'The richer the sensorimotor engagement that a reader experiences with a text, the greater the opportunities for multisensory information encoding and for the text to be comprehended'. The book with its 'four corners and a frame', allows a reader to 'see where a piece of textual information is in relation to the page corners and borders' (Hou et al. 2017).

125
In accordance with original data collection, responses from the photobook reading survey are not attributed to specific readers.

photobook runs deep into our experiences, but far more difficult is to witness or theorise what happens when it sits on our desk, shelf or bedside table. This less involved engagement with the book beyond reading relies on its material properties, just as our haptic engagement does. The physical book must be stored in some way by its reader, archivist or custodian, and, unlike a digital work, it is common that this placement will allow for regular engagement by the eye and mind, if not the hand. The photobook's residence on the floor or a desk, or placement beside other works in a chronological or arbitrary fashion, throws up new readings without opening the book itself — new proximities that are begun physically and become mental. This reading of the book shares similarities with the way in which Jean Baudrillard speaks about how the objects he possesses become 'mental precincts over which I hold sway, they become things of which I am the meaning' (2005, 91).[126] This 'sway' might be exhibited simply in the personal connections we make with books, but can also be seen more overtly in the positioning of a title on a bookshelf, re-reading or its lending and gifting.

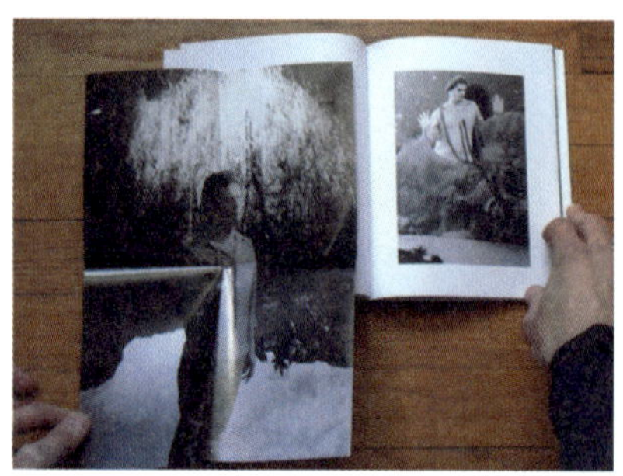

⤶ Jörg Colberg undertaking a video reading of Anouk Kruithof's *A Head with Wings* (2011). Image courtesy of Jörg Colberg.

As we organise (or refuse to organise) our photobooks, they are moved away from their positions as a product of the maker to a product of the reader. We bring meaning to works in the swapping, borrowing and lending we conduct — bundling them with some of the meaning we have made in their company, introducing and recommending new works to new people. And, it is in these actions that the photobook, or any book for that matter, breaks free of its temporary physical inertia (see 'Photobooks & access').

126
This notion of sway echoes in artist Eric van Der Weijde's notes when he speaks of decontextualisation — 'The book, as an object, gains strength as it gets decontextualised by its viewer, owner, or bookcase in which it stands' (van Der Weijde 2018, 145). For van der Weijde, it is the removal of the publication from its contextual location of production that is lost, but its contextual location of reception that gives it new strength.

↳ Looking at the photobook as a montage

Having detailed several notable facets of the photobook-as-object, we can turn to the photobook as a sequence of spaces. In looking at a reading of the medium in this manner, I reiterate a core principal that harks back to Alex Sweetman's proposal in 1985 for the 'photobookwork', which is not a 'portfolio between covers' but 'a series of images ... in a linear sequence' (Sweetman 1985, 187), and in turn to Ulises Carrión speaking in 1975 about the artist's book, pioneered by poets:

> 'A sequence of spaces.
> Each of these spaces is perceived
> at a different moment
> – a book is also a sequence of moments.
> A book is not a case of words, nor a bag of words,
> nor a bearer of words' (Carrión 2018, 27).

To begin a comprehension of what occurs when separate images (even those constructed in different times, and with different means in mind) come together, there are few clearer presentations than Takeshi Kitano's narrative game[127] featured in the 600th edition of *Cahiers du Cinéma*. Kitano demonstrated the arbitrary and necessary elements of the sequence, which are 'arbitrary, because there is no evident connection between the images in a given narrative; necessary because once the images are grouped there appears to be a connection (causation, linearity)' (Rohdie 2006, 7). The narratives constructed relied on the image as a 'document' and the constructed narrative as 'pure contrivance ... real without being true ... belonging at once to fact and imagination' (Rohdie 2006, 8).

In Kitano's game, a suggested narrative could be formed via consequential progression from one image to the next, or in the space between images in the sequence. The former of these approaches is Kuleshovian[128] — constructed 'brick by brick' in order to form meaning. In this way, the sequence resembles a journey, with each image delivering a new detail for the reader to add in. But this alone is not enough to account for

127
Kitano's process was to take an initial set of 69 images and from this set, create mini-narratives of four. He produced 14, and an additional 16 were produced by other film-makers; a set, then, of 30 narratives, each comprising four images and each using as their only source the original 69 photographs.

128
Named after Soviet filmmaker and theorist Lev Kuelshov. A book like Watabe Yukichi's *A Criminal Investigation* (2011) is a good example of this formation of sequence, as we follow a detective investigating a murder.

how meaning is formed in the photobook. Few contemporary works provide such apparently chronologically organised images, and as the graphical elicitation responses later in this chapter show, not all readers will travel through a book from cover to cover in order. Here, Sergei Eisenstein's emphasis on the clash, rather than construction, of meaning is helpful. Writing about film montage, Eisenstein proposed that when images are placed together, a 'collision' and 'conflict' occurs (Eisenstein in Rohdie 2006, 87). He proposed that alongside meaning made brick-by-brick, it is also found within this energetic coming together of visuals. For Eisenstein, neither the 'previous' nor 'next' image give anything to one another. Instead, both lend themselves to a space of conflict, which rather than being on the screen or page, is in the mind of the reader. Eisenstein's own examples could quite readily be photographic:

> 'a mouth + a child = "to scream";
> a mouth + a bird = "to sing";
> a knife + a heart = "sorrow"' (Eisenstein 1977, 30).

Where film theory loses relevancy to the photobook, however, is in its inability to deal with a user-operated and user-navigated medium like the book. Unlike a cinematic audience whose time and pace of watching is 'controlled by the film', for the photobook 'it is the spectator who "animates" the pictures' (Bate 2014, 54). In this way, the medium more closely resembles the interactions we might have with the novel or poem, served by literary theory.

↳ Reading the photobook as a text

A timeline of modern literature can be broadly described as the progression from a fascination with the unique view of the author, to exclusive interest in the text, before – only in the later stages of the 20th century – considering the reader (Eagleton 1994, 74).

There is of course more to be found in the details,[129] but I mention this timeline because it echoes some of what can be seen in photobook criticism — with the latter, reader-focused period yet to arrive. Looking closer, we can see the first parallel to photobook reading in formalism. Formalism adopts a position in which meaning is derived solely from within the work at hand, and does not rely on external texts or structures. The text is considered as 'an autonomous object divorced from the specific circumstances of its creation and creator, and from the historical and social context of its reception' (Cook 1995, 130). With the photobook in mind, these elements might be replaced by a dissection of the rhythm, flow, pace and aesthetics of the work. This formalist approach to the book has been encouraged in part by the photobook-as-art discourse spoken of in 'Photobooks & community', and a maker-dominated audience for whom the inner workings of the book are important reference points. It is a reading that can be found in many photographic departments, in education as well as reviews, in Jörg Colberg's photobook taxonomy (2018) and several responses to the photobook reading survey:

> 'First I would look at the pictures but not in the linear order, then I would read the text and then I would look at the pictures in the linear order trying to understand why a particular picture was chosen and why the pictures are in that particular order.'

Alongside[130] readings that interrogate the text isolated from its context, are readings that highlight connections with an artist's oeuvre, a publisher's catalogue, world events or aesthetically similar works. Such readings we can align with a structuralist approach. Structuralists look for underlying connections in the work that relate to structures of a group of texts, as well as structures lying outside of the work: means of production, time of production, genre, political systems and so on (Cook 1995, 141). For the photobook,

129
Like the cultural studies strands of literary theory that have helped position feminist literary criticism, queer theory, postcolonial criticism and ecocriticism as contemporary tools of the reader and critic.

130
It is important to note that adopting a formalist approach to reading, or any other for that matter, does not prohibit alternative approaches to reading (even of the same book).

often it is the blurb, précis or publisher's description of a given work that encourages a structuralist approach, as in this example, where RVB Books frame a reading of Oscar Monzón's work *Karma* (2013):

> 'Never fabricated, these photos, most of which we can imagine were stolen, refer to Luc Boltanski's concept of "body car". Being the only object which both completely absorbs us and that we can manipulate at our own will from the inside, cars cause a sensation of passing elsewhere with a sense of security. They offer a private space among the midst of a public sphere and create a familiar realm which permits the most private experiences' (RVB Books 2016).

Structuralism requires an investigation that goes beyond the single text. It asks of those using it (consciously or not) that they must be well-read — familiar with the time of publication, political landscape, comparative works and so on. While not explicit, the subtext of these accompaniments to photobooks is that the work would not have been fully realised or understood by the reader if they had not identified these connections: a key tenet of the structuralists' argument in literary theory. A structuralist approach to the photobook is visible in many photobook reviews[131] (often alongside formalism), artists' and publishers' statements, and it is present too in the photobook reading survey.[132] There is, though, another group of responses to the survey that neither formalism nor structuralism is able to represent. These are responses that speak from a subjective, experiential position, a position from which literary theory shied away, and even explicitly rejected, until the later stages of the 20th century (Bennett and Royle, 2009, 11).

131
A book of the week on the Photo-Eye blog, *12Hz* by Ron Jude (2020) was read by Blake Andrews: 'With cloth binding, tipped-in cover image, lush sweeping reproductions, and quietly dignified elegance, *12 Hz* feels closer to Awoiska van der Molen than Vitreous China. Jude has left behind the wry social commentary of previous works, choosing instead a more rarified and refined direction. It's a nice twist in the oeuvre from a photographer who consistently pushes himself into new territory.'

132
'I open the cover, look for the colophon, find out where it was printed, who by, who helped make it etc. Who it is by is less important. My first thought is, when did this come out, how was it produced, where was it produced? These things will all influence my reading.'

↳ Constructing a unique reading

> 'I turn the pages slowly in sequence from beginning to end. I tend not to read any text or captions. I keep checking in with what (if any) emotional reaction I'm experiencing; questioning why.'

The role of the reader as an active meaning-maker is something that has appeared in several writings on reading the photobook (and artist's book) that I encountered in my research. In Joanna Cresswell and Oliver Whitehead's *Some Thoughts*, they describe readers via a list of roles they perform, and in doing so begin to elevate and visualise their position in relation to the photobook: 'Readers actively participate, look, exchange, borrow, give, take, steal, feedback' (2015, 26–7). This conversational, back and forth with the book is present too in the essay *Liminal Moments at the Edges: Reading Montage Narratives in Artists' Books*, in which Victoria Cooper explores the connection between maker and reader and the resulting 'collaboration' of a specific reading (2019, 17). The sentiment is also mirrored in Alejandro Acin's comment that reading the photobook is akin to 'directing a movie with someone else's script'. As an example, in the following extract where Tate Shaw reflects upon a sequence of images in Gregory Halpern's *A* (2011) we can clearly see the points at which Shaw moves from describing the sequence (reading the script) to constructing its meaning (directing):

> 'It starts on the cover with a photo of hands holding an x-ray signifying injury. With the memory of the x-ray in your mind, you then engage with overlaid and inverted maps, suggesting an excursion through multiple injured, damaged cities ... A lot where a house was demolished, followed by a house with a hole in the side, then another patched house, then a bush we could hide within, fort-like. This is about our basic need for shelter. These

> photos represent the housing crisis, the great recession, the blight in the urban core of our small cities' (Shaw 2012, 4).

Designer, publisher and photographer Valentina Abenavoli describes images as being 'at the viewer's disposal and imagination', with their meanings losing 'capacity for unilateral power and presence' (2019, 28). The photobook, then, can be viewed as a series of potential spaces, suspended in quantum narratives that are constructed from two sides of the book. On one side the makers construct a sequence of spaces in order to convey meaning, whilst on the other, readers construct their own sequence of spaces, which may lead to a very different, and always unique, experience.[133]

This quantum-ness of the photobook extends beyond sequence and is influenced by more than our direct reading. It is also found in the research a reader may undertake before encountering a work, whether they may read an essay that precedes the images or not, or whether they progress through a work in a linear fashion, are all part of reading and its results. As we can see from these two responses regarding approaches to reading in the survey, there are many permutations in picking up the photobook:

> '[I start by] looking at the cover front and back, considering the outer design. Then I tend to quickly flick through the book, followed by slowly viewing the work in order, sometimes going back to particular images, thinking about the design, sequencing, edit, paper. I will always read the essay or text after I've viewed the work in its entirety.'

> 'I inspect the binding and construction for clues how to handle it. Then begin with any forward text for guides from the artist or publisher on how to go about reading it. If the second part isn't included, then I'll just start leafing through.'

133
Keith Smith offers a succinct summary in his use of the terms 'random' and 'directed' referral. For Smith, the 'random referral' is a free association made by the viewer, and 'directed referral' is an intentional relationship set up by the picture maker (Smith 1994, 105).

‘By holding together images of a sequence the photobook accommodates the quest for immersion in a perfect way. It supplies a unique experience, as a single beholder usually looks at it. This person can take her own time to look at the images, to study them, to immerse herself in them; this person decides when to move forward, when to turn back, and how long and how often the photographs are looked at. The medium of the photobook is able to create an intimate togetherness of the book and its beholder.’ (Lockemann 2014, 126)

Fig. 11

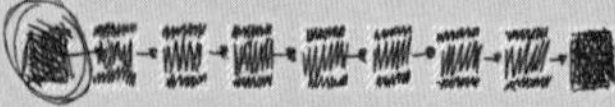

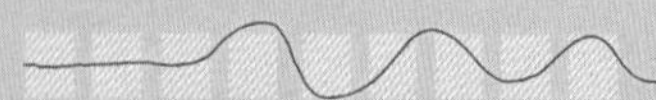

There are those who encounter a new photobook and progress through in a linear manner ...

Those who flit from page to page ...

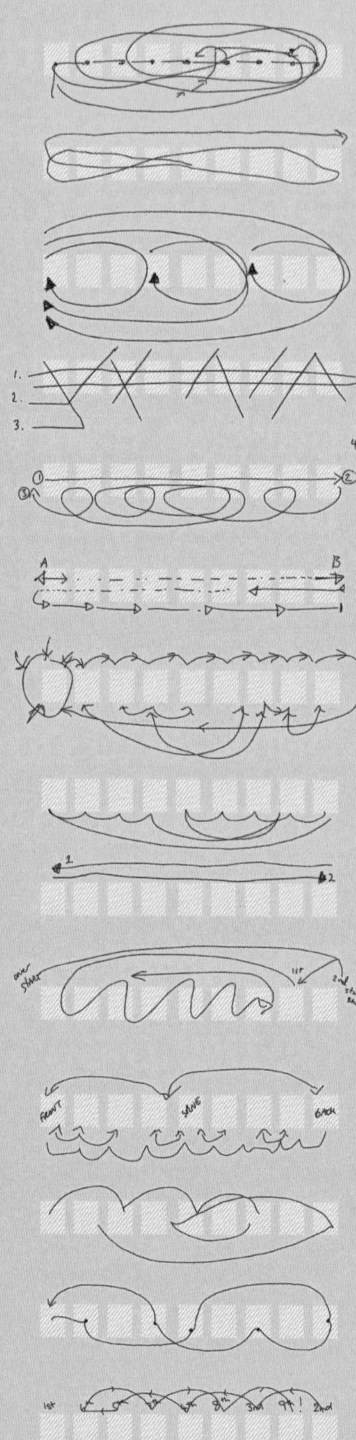

And then the largest group, who undertake a multi-directional reading that could be described as repetitive or circular, though many of these examples still exhibit an element of linearity.

Though the ways in which to travel through a sequence of pages are almost infinite, there are some patterns and commonalities in engagement. Their identification comes from a piece of research I conducted from 2016–17 with 27 individuals who represent a cross-section of the photobook community, made up of students, teachers, designers, photographers and publishers, employing graphical elicitation as a way to visualise navigation of the photobook.

These responses highlight the individuality of reading, and with it, accentuate the enormous role that readers, even in their approach to navigation, undertake. What follows is a proposal for eight acts of photobook reading that recognises this individuality, and allows us to map out our experiences with photobooks from before they arrive in our hands, to the stretched out reading of their lives on shelves and tables. Of primary consideration in the construction of these acts is that they are informed by research: in encountered literature, data collection and interviews. Paramount too is that they offer an inclusive account of reading and should not create a hierarchy of reading by suggesting good, or bad, reading.[134]

134
This hierarchy is unhelpful in looking beyond an insular audience for the photobook ('Photobooks & community') but is already present in photobook discourse, typified by comments like those of Gerry Badger in his article on reading the photobook in *The Photobook Review* (2013):

'One might take the analogy between a good and a bad symphony conductor. The bad conductor treats the score primarily on a visceral level, treating each passage, a tune or phrase, as an episode in itself. The good conductor is aware of the music's intellectual as well as its visceral qualities. He gets the most out of each passage, of course, but also treats the work as a whole and not just the sum of its parts, pointing out its overarching structure' (Badger 2011, 3).

↳ Eight acts of photobook reading

I Distance reading: the reading that comes before any physical encounter with a photobook. This includes our existing knowledge about the publisher, designer or photographer, but also includes information about the book itself gleaned from blogs, retail spaces and social media. This reading is exemplified by comments like:

> 'Sometimes I get enthusiastic after reading a good review and decide to buy without having had a physical experience with a book beforehand. Most often it's a network of influences. In recent

> years I more readily buy books by publishers and photographers/artists I know or am friends with.'
>
> 'A book or photographer I know from previous experience or reputation will mean I have preconceived ideas about what to expect and the complexity of the visual language.'

Distance reading is a space in which the information that accompanies a publication has considerable bearing, as does the conversation that surrounds it, and the reader's prior knowledge of the makers' work — all of which may inform subsequent acts.

II Material reading: includes a physical and haptic inspection of the book as an object and signifier of the work within. This means that not only will size, shape and texture be considered, but also the colour, font and any graphic display information. This reading is exemplified by comments like:

> 'I feel the paper
> I look at the front and back cover
> I look at the finishing.'
>
> 'I would probably hold the book in my hands first to familiarise myself with its tactile aspects. I would then open it up and flick through its pages at random.'

In some readings, this act will offer clues as to the content or intent of the work, in others it may be with a view to the reader's own experiments with book production and in many it may also be an unconscious act.

III Inspectional reading: building on material reading, here the reader opens the book and begins to form a loose picture of the work in the mind. This inspectional reading is not by any means thorough — it is in some ways similar to the act of reading a single page of a novel from the first chapter. The reader looks to get a sense of the style of the writing/work as a way to decide how, and if, they might progress with their reading.[135] This reading is exemplified by comments like:

> 'I flip through pages from back to front, turn it and weigh it in my hands, flip through the first pages and if I like it, continue.'

> 'Front cover, back cover, weight, format, a first fast reading to feel the rhythm, a second slower reading of text (if present).'

IV Navigational reading: a navigational reading can range from the linear journey through the book to the multi-directional reading seen in the graphical elicitation responses. It may also span from a relatively passive spectatorship of image progression, to an active consideration of the montage elements in the work. If a re-reading is to occur, it is likely that the shape of this act will be considerably different. This reading is exemplified by comments like:

> 'I start at the beginning, generally skipping any text, and flip through the book at a reasonably quick pace.'

> 'I flick through, stop at images that grab me, read any text (short in length) that can give the book context written by the artist, then go through page by page in order.'

V Conceptual reading: typically operating in tandem with act IV,[136] conceptual reading is an analytical and reflective process that looks to understand why or how the work is constructed in the manner it is. This act is thus considerably influenced by the intent of reading as much as the intent of the work at hand (see 'Photobooks & intent'). This reading is exemplified by comments like:

135
This reading is a very specific act that will often only serve as a way to decide whether further acts will be engaged with, or whether this is in fact the end of the reading. It is possible that these inspectional acts will be less overt, in particular if a reader has been gifted a work or asked to look at it. Even here, though, initial impressions are formed before a navigational reading.

136
Typified in many comments like: 'First I would look at the pictures but not in the linear order, then I would read the text and then I would look at the pictures in the linear order trying to understand why a particular picture was chosen and why the pictures are in that particular order.'

> 'First of all I just glance in the book to explore it and know what kind of photographic work I'm going to face. After that I try to take my time to follow the sequence and figure out the main idea.'

> 'A new photobook is like the beginning of a trip through the narrative of its author, following, trying to understand where he/she is going.'

VI Assimilatory reading: here, the findings from previous readings are comparatively analysed (consciously or not) with existing knowledge and awareness of other works, situations and experiences. Again, the intent of a reading is significant in this act. Thus, a photographer working towards publishing his or her own book will extrapolate and assimilate in a different manner from the student asked to locate a book in a specific historical context, or the Hong Kong resident gifted a book about the anti-extradition law.[137] This reading is exemplified by comments like:

> 'I tend to connect it with other works, sometimes by other authors or even my own work. Sometimes I also play at imagining how the very same book (with the same images) could have been different.'

> 'When the book cover is closed, there's the moment of reflection and attempt to engage with what it was that I just experienced, what was the meaningfulness of that, and how I internalise that.' (Doug Spowart).

VII Shelf-reading: this reading is the least definable of all — it exists beyond the concentrated reading above, and essentially refers to any interaction with the book after stages I-VI and which cannot be described as 're-reading' (to follow). There will be many works that are never re-read in a concentrated manner, but may be turned over in the hand or simply considered from a distance — this I categorise as shelf-reading.[138]

137
Assimilatory reading can be seen as structuralist due to the way in which it forges connections with texts outside of the one that is being read. But I do not wish to prescribe the need for awareness of other photobooks or art texts. Assimilation with lived experience, current affairs, relationships or the self are all valid outcomes of this act.

138
An interesting project that asks for a shelf reading in order to ascertain our reading bias is Related Tactics' *Shelf Life* of 2019, an invitation to reflect on our bookshelves using stickers that highlight some connections, biases and preferences. Ultimately, this direct intervention on our shelves asks if the voices and perspectives we have encountered are diverse, or if our 'collected knowledge may be incomplete' (Related Tactics 2019).

Shelf-reading takes note of the placement of books but also the effect they have as we pass them, lend them to others or revisit them. This reading is exemplified by comments regarding organisation of books like:

> 'Books by same artist grouped together where possible. Books of the same size grouped together. And bookshelf arranged with consideration to spine colour tones and themes.'

> 'Sometimes I'll just grab something off a shelf, flick through it for a few seconds, simply because it caught my eye and I'd not thought about that book for a while.'

VIII Re-reading: to attempt to summarise any return to a book for more than a shelf-read is bold indeed, but the clear difference in attitude and experience of re-reading from both the survey and interviews shows that there is merit in separating it. Re-reading is any engagement with a book that comes after the reading acts presented to this point — this is the only space in which it can occur, since it relies on existing reading acts to navigate its 'post' position. This act may occur in a search for something in particular (research/to lend/show) or the familiar return to a favourite work:

> 'I feel that with a book that I've owned for longer, I'll spend a longer amount of time with it as it has a bond with me that will always be explored. Yet with a newer book, there's some sort of resistance about what to expect, so there's more of a critical nature about reading.'

> 'Re-reading a photobook for me is more like a walk in a beautiful place I've been before and chosen to come to again.'

> 'I go back to older [photobooks] with specific goals in mind; images or physical characteristics.'

Worth highlighting is the last comment, which emphasises that while re-reading implies a return to the same text, it is not in any sense a repetition of a previous version. Re-reading may well circle back to the navigational, or conceptual, or yet further to the inspectional, but it is typically noticeably different the second time around.[139] Just as with shelf-reading, it is unhelpful to prescribe the shapes or approaches of this reading, and more fruitful to note that it will adopt the characteristics of the act to which it is returned.

These acts of reading are constructed in a linear order, but could be reworked with the removal or accentuation of some acts, to allow for broad approaches to the photobook. The order of acts represents the increasing transference of meaning-construction in the book: from the maker to the reader. At the beginning of our acts, it is predominantly the makers who are able to inform and shape our interactions. It is the makers (or other makers in the photobook community) who will often inform our distance reading and it is the maker's physical construction of a work that will shape the haptic inspection of material reading. At inspectional reading, in which the reader performs a brief analysis of the content of the work, a judgment of the work is made and the active reader enters into the process in a more pronounced way.[140] Through the middle acts (navigational and conceptual), the maker and reader work together in the construction of meaning via collaboration (Cooper 2019), with the reader navigating the book and often simultaneously decoding or interrogating the pages.

As we approach assimilatory reading, it is now the reader who is the primary producer of meaning. They are still working from an experience orchestrated in part by the maker, but it is an act so far removed from the maker's control, and so personal, that it is the reader who is dominant. This continues as the book is stored and displayed (shelf reading) and returned

139
Evidenced by my graphical elicitation exercises, which were repeated for a return reading (not shown here), as well as the original presented in figure 11, where a new book was read.

140
Though the reader 'takes over' the photobook, the influence of the maker, the maker-centric discourse and de-functionalisation of the photobook that have been explored in 'Photobooks & community' and 'Photobooks & access' may well slow or control this to a certain degree. Similarly, while distance reading may be shaped by reviews, blurbs and the look or content of a given work, it is still the reader who choses to pick it up or order it.

Fig. 12

Distance reading
The information we gather consciously or collect unconsciously prior to picking up the book or entering a first reading.

Material reading
A brief material consideration of the photobook.

Inspectional reading
A brief consideration of the photobook's contents and non-material form.

Navigational reading
An investigation of content, which may be either passive and spectator-like, or active and scholarly.

Conceptual reading
A questioning of the purpose of the work — why does it operate in this manner? What is being communicated?

Assimilatory reading
Making connections to other works, experiences, actions and relationships.

Shelf-reading
The physical positioning of the photobook and its connection to an ongoing cognitive connection with the work.

Re-reading
Any secondary reading of a work, which can be begun after any act.

to in the future (re-reading). The book is now truly an object over which readers hold 'sway' and to which they 'bring meaning' (Baudrillard 2005 91).

Acts of reading provide a structure for the photobook maker, reader and critic to consider — a tool that articulates the parameters of most interactions with the medium, and can offer a series of areas in which to invest time and thought. By clearly articulating a process of reading, we can use it, together with other aids in this book, to more robustly and appropriately understand and critiquc works. What's more, we may be able to combine these acts with the discussion of amplification and activation in 'Photobooks & access' to construct spaces and environments that facilitate, highlight or reflect upon particular acts.[141]

Acts of reading I hope will challenge the prevalence of a maker-centric discourse. In a subtle manner, their incorporation into our lexicon could allow non-maker readers to be heard, and in turn provide a space for them around the table of the new photobook. So much of the photobook's life is in the hands of the reader, but it is a part of the medium that until now we have considered very little. A discourse that is better balanced to include the reader acknowledges and relishes the potentiality of communication through the photobook, and the action of the reader, who is as much responsible for constructing meaning as the maker. It is hoped that the research-informed acts of reading I have presented here, whether used strictly or in the abstract, may support new conversations that will provide scaffolding for a more inclusive, and even potent, medium.

141
Anshika Varma provided postcards on which readers could write after engaging with books in her pop-up libraries. The idea was intended to 'allow the readers a moment after going through the book to sit down in one place and maybe assimilate what they've taken from the book.' This can be seen as a reification of assimilatory reading.

This chapter touched briefly on literary theory, something that was a more prominent part of my PhD thesis. Broad texts like Sara Upstone's *Literary Theory: A Complete Introduction* (2017) and Terry Eagleton's *Literary Theory: An Introduction* (2010) are good places to start for those interested in this area, with publications from Roland Barthes (1977) Wolfgang Iser (1995), Jane Tompkins (1980) and Andrew Bennett all offering more in relation to the reader's place in the text, which became popular to consider at the end of the last century. Alberto Manguel's *A History of Reading* (1997) is a thorough and insightful work, which offers so many avenues to explore — historical and (relatively) contemporary. Katherine Hayles' writing in *Electronic Literature: New Horizons for the Literary* (2008), *How we Think: Digital Media and Contemporary Technogenesis* (2012) and *Writing Machines* (2002) present a rewarding digital tangent, that can provide ways to think about the haptic book in relation to electronic counterparts.

For those interested in Tim Daly's approach to reading the physical artist's book, and the significance of touch in *Book Handling as a Research Method*, it may be helpful to consider terminology. The book, and in particular the photobook, has a complex relationship with haptics that spans what might be termed *haptic poetry, haptic technology* and *haptic sensing* (or haptic perception). These may be useful for those investigating the area.

The photobook reading reflections of Valentina Abenavoli in *Swaying Time on a Flatland* (2019), Joanna Cresswell and Oliver Whitehead's *The Photobook: Some Thoughts* (2015) and Doug Spowart's *Ten Steps: 'Reading a Photobook'* (2016) are useful resources to encourage research and thought in different directions. Victoria Cooper's *Liminal Moments at the Edges:*

Reading Montage Narratives in Artists' Books (2019) can also aid investigation with a tendency towards montage and sequence, alongside the collection of essays in Gerry Badger's *Imprint: Visual Narratives in Books and Beyond* (2013). Shelly Rice's essay *Words and Images: Artists' Books as Visual Literature* (1985) is worth seeking out (especially since it is found alongside numerous other great writings in Joan Lyon's *Artists' Books: A Critical Anthology and Sourcebook*. Briony Carlin's upcoming doctoral thesis on the 'materiality and social agency of contemporary photobooks' and the 'ways in which [they] affect us in emotional and multi-sensory capacities' I am sure will be a significant contribution to the field and an essential resource — something to look out for. The reader may also wish to seek out two of Tate Shaw's essay's found in *Blurred Library* (2016) — the first, which deals with the comfort and containment of the finite book, is called *Reading as Prowling, Book as Cage*, and the second, which looks at sequence (and is referenced in this chapter) is called *Strategic Linkage* and considers in some depth Gregory Halpern's *A*, a photobook from 2011.

Lastly, released as a 30-minute film in April 2021, *Photobook: The Book Club Test* is a fascinating watch and wonderful experiment. In it, Source photographic review gave three 'classic photobooks'[142] to two reading groups (who typically discuss the novel). The resulting conversations demonstrate many of the acts seen in my account of reading, and highlight the connections and discrepancies between the three experts[143] reflections on the books, and that of the book club members themselves.

142
Robert Frank's *The Americans*, Stephen Shore's *Uncommon Places* and Nan Goldin's *The Ballad of Sexual Dependency.*

143
Caroline Blinder, David Campany and Catherine Grant.

Photobooks & the future

Driven by a dedicated community, the contemporary photobook has ascended to a position of prominence in photography. This rise has enabled, and been enabled by, new photobook histories, medium-specific communities and the legitimisation of the photobook as its own medium. So, where to next? Can what we have learned in the post-millennium assist the construction of a sustainable future? What place might the reader have in building a new discourse and ecology? How do we address issues of access to the book and its contents? It will be us, the makers and members of the photobook community who will ultimately decide how our vibrant medium progresses.

↳ Productive ascent, critical plateau

The swell of activity around the photobook that has been seen in this book ('Photobooks & community') has been changing over the last five years. Dedicated blogs have reduced in the vigour of their output or stopped entirely, regularly updated collections have been taken into institutional spaces[144] and many small publishers have been discontinued.[145] Some of the energy and excitement that gave rise to the boom of the contemporary photobook has dispersed, and in turn, conversations around the medium have begun to shift.[146] The Photobook Club presents a useful barometer for the changing shape of the photobook ecology, with many communities reducing in scale, stopping events for long periods of time or focusing energies on other projects. Both Juan Cires (PBC Madrid) and Jon Uriarte (PBC Barcelona) attribute this to the increasing number of spaces and resources to which people can turn for support in comprehending the medium — something they saw as a real need that the project met in its infancy.

> 'At the beginning it was quite crazy and I had to set up a limit of people because the events were too long. It started really strongly and I think there was a real need for something like this. In my last few meetings it wasn't so crowded and it went up and down a little after that. Right at the beginning, around 2011, 2012, 2013, was the height I would say' (Jon Uriarte).

> 'The Photobook Club came around at a time when the photobook was becoming really big in photography and a lot of people were thinking about the photobook and what it is ... Once the photobook became a part of the photography world and there were other resources available for people to look at, and other spaces to learn about the photobook, then The Photobook Club becomes less important' (Juan Cires).

144
Such as the Indie Photobook Library now residing in the Beinecke rare book and manuscript collection at Yale University, and the Self Publish, Be Happy collection now housed at the Maison Européenne de la Photographie in Paris.

145
'Photobook workshops, events, festivals, awards and fairs took over the scene, while publishing didn't manage to become a sustainable business. This doesn't necessarily reflect the status of "independence", in a broader sense, it relates to a market that stays niche — with its positive and negative turns' (Salvatore Vitale in Vitale et al. 2020).

146
There have been several acceptances of the photobook's momentum slowing, or at least its activity morphing, with Tate Shaw noting that since a zenith in 2015/16 it hasn't 'seemed as interesting to just talk about books for books' sake', with so much else going on in the world.

If activity and action in the early days of the contemporary photobook has led to a more established medium, with resources and networks that simply didn't exist before the millennium, we might expect a better-equipped and similarly energised continuation, but it has not fully materialised. Bruno Ceschel of Self Publish, Be Happy suggests that this gradual descent may be due to a lack of a replacement generation to take over, and that this can be attributed in part to a changing economic situation, which doesn't allow for the same risks to be taken.[147] But Ceschel sees the positives too — in the sense that it is always a good result when an 'element of any vanguard is absorbed into the mainstream'. Certainly it is hard to see how the photobook would return to its former status now that we have a far better understanding of its histories, production and content.

Quite what the legacy of this exciting time will be, or what the absorbed elements of the vanguard are, remains to be seen, but already a more reflective and critical environment is showing signs of life. In 2018, Ceschel instigated the *Photobook:RESET* event in Berlin, whereby a range of participants were brought together to address a series of pressing issues for the medium.[148] Then, in 2020, *The Photobook in Art and Society* was published, with a clear agenda to think of the codex as a valuable communication form beyond our limited community. What Ruth Gilberger makes clear in this publication (itself born from experiments with public engagement with the photobook), is that the format has great 'participative potential' to help to make our world 'visible, understandable and alterable' (Gilberger 2020, 32):

> 'As a hybrid medium the photobook not only illustrates, in the truest sense of the word, complex contexts with regards to reality; it can also make them readable and tangible in the condensed form of a book' (Gilberger 2020, 28).

147
In the UK, for example, tuition has risen from £0 per year at the start of the millennium, to over £9,000 in 2020. Together with the removal of maintenance grants (replaced by loans), it means that the average student debt is £44,000.

148
Many of the issues *Photobook:RESET* addressed have been present in my own research, and in these pages — 'Is our close-knit community of like-minded people its own limit? Who is the photobook for? Indeed, is the photobook as we know it even an effective form of communication?' (Self Publish, Be Happy 2018).

There is, then, a growing acceptance of a need to reflect on what it is we do with the photobook,[149] and how to look to a more sustainable (and I would posit more purposeful) future. Simultaneously, the gentle decline in noise around the medium presents an environment that is perhaps more conducive to perspectives that may have been seen as counter or alternative to the omnipresence of celebratory and contributive discourse. There are numerous possible ways in which we may look to posit a strong future for the photobook, but I suggest that many of them can be contained within the establishing of a reading economy.

↳ A reading economy

What I present is a proposal — rooted in the explorations of this book — for a shifting of attention, action, and acknowledgment, from the production of works, to their reception. It is hoped that, as we find ourselves on a plateau, or slight descent from 'photobibliomania' (Solo and the Library of the International Centre of Photography 2014), we can construct a reading economy rather than a maker-centric production economy, and that in doing so, a subtle transformation in production itself occurs, from making, to making public. If we do adopt a shift of attention, what might it look like?

A *reading economy* (a term used by Stadler 2018, 118–27 that I extend here) is one that would elevate considerations of the pragmatics of making public, and would strive to produce for readerships a work with identified and practical price-points, haptic qualities, contextual information and visual language. Decisions in production would be met following these parameters, and while this imposes limits, they will be of varying degrees according to the intent of publishing. For many makers, this may seem identical to their current manner of operation, but when we simultaneously challenge the fact that the core (and often only) readership is

149 Conversations around activist publishing and political photobooks were present at both the Contemporary Artists' Book conference and the Photobook Sessions conference in 2021. In the former, these conversations were more focused and overt, whereas the latter was still dominated by talk of design, production and photographic content. Nevertheless, there is evidence of an increasingly self-critical discourse.

like-minded makers, the equations take on new significance. A reading economy is one in which the photobook maker is acutely aware of the need to amplify and activate the social life of the book in order to locate and bring together a public for the work's reception. Stadler makes the case that passivity will not suffice:

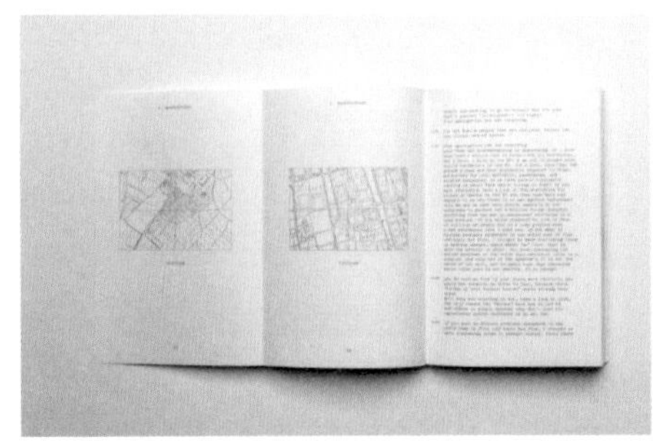

> 'Publics begin in wilful actions, an invitation, an event. A public can arise in any defined space that is open to strangers — a street, a meeting hall, a plaza or bar, or a book' (Stadler 2018, 122).

There are echoes here of the intention with which The Photobook Club launched, and has continued to develop, as well as a reminder that key for the photobook (which is a medium already wieldable by large publics)[150] is the need for amplification and activation, deliberate choices rather than passive proposals: a set of 'wilful actions'. Establishing a reading economy does not create a simplified, algorithmic production methodology seeking only to be popular with readers, but addresses the power imbalance in the photobook's possibilities that live in the space between maker and reader. As the role, voice and location of the reader becomes clearer in photobook discourse, a number of problematics encountered in this publication are mitigated or challenged.[151]

Whilst a reading economy is a proposal for the future of the photobook, it seeks to take with it the many wonderful publications produced since the millennium that may have been swallowed up in a frantic abundance of works, and have not fully realised their potential. *Republication* is one way in which to revitalise them, and even for those works that were reader-focused may re-form conversations in a new context.[152] Republication is not to be confused with a second printing. Instead, all of the minutiae contained within

150
In that both photography and the book are media that are well known and understood for common use by the very vast majority of the global population.

151
As an example, the esoteric and production-driven discourse of review may morph into a reflection on reception and the efficacy of the book to bring readers together, impart ideas or spark conversation.

152
Nicolo Degiorgis' *Hidden Islam, 479 comments* (2014b) is an interesting work to think of here. This publication was a follow-up to *Hidden Islam* (2014a) and featured no photographs. Instead, comments were used from a *Guardian* article in which the original book (of makeshift sites of worship in Italy) was reviewed. Degiorgis frames the second publication as part of an approach that starts, rather than stops, with the original publication: '*I always saw Hidden Islam* as a starting point for extending the discussion ... Even though the second book does not contain photographs as such, it is still conceptually a photograph, a snapshot of what people think about immigration' (O'Hagan 2015).

← Nicolo Degiorgis' *Hidden Islam, 479 Comments* (2014). Image courtesy of the artist.

the act of publishing must once again be encountered and reflected upon in relation to the reader. The result for some could be a series of events around the original work or a companion text, whereas for others it might be a change in geographical distribution, a digital counterpart or a series of recorded conversations. Regardless, the choice of republishing is one born of action and intent on behalf of the photobook maker.[153]

> 'To republish is to work against the invisibility of objects and information by extracting them from the fabric of the real or of history in order to summon them, show them again, and open up the field of their potential readings' (Bobin and Villeneuve 2012, 16).

Bobin and Villeneuve's call for re-opening is an act that stems from a conviction that there is a 'responsibility' for the maker to 'reinsert the object into the public sphere' (2012, 18), a belief that I suggest may be latent or temporarily obfuscated in the climate of the contemporary photobook. *Photobooks &* has found evidence of strong connections between the photobook and its community, built on maker-centrism ('Photobooks & community'), an emphasis on the quality and sophistication of production ('Photobooks and access') and the unification of histories of intent under the 'photobook' banner ('Photobooks & intent'), but these traits of the medium construct restrictions and miss connections with readers unfamiliar with the contemporary form, including those who are often represented within its pages. With practicality, action and intent core to this publication, what steps can we take to encourage a reading economy?

153
Tiffany Jones: 'To me, the stories are living, they don't end, and so there's an opportunity to take it somewhere else and try and makes it accessible to different people. And it works as far as we've seen ... I personally think that reprinting a book in the same manner is a lost opportunity. I think you can enrich the story by making a variation.

↳ A critical framework

The framework I include here (see figure 13) is the product of the central themes of this book (and the research from which it stems), constructed from encountered literature, case studies and most importantly, perspectives from the field in the many interviews conducted as part of my work. I see the framework's merit as lying in its simplicity and applicability for the maker, as well as for those coming to the photobook with a critical eye, who contribute to current photobook discourse.[154] Its use is intended as strictly practical: to support a line of questioning and provide scaffolding and vocabulary that can be used to begin critical conversations that go beyond material, haptic or aesthetic qualities — ultimately seeking to understand and extend connections between makers and readers.

The critical framework addresses and activates the space between maker and reader in which the photobook resides. It begins from the maker's perspective with a recognition of the intent of publishing or (if desired) the possibility of alignment of their work with a particular lineage.[155] Unlike all other stages of the framework, which both inform and are informed by their counterparts, intent of publishing only informs that which follows. Thus, when production is arrived at, this stage should reflect and respond to a purpose of publishing.[156] The book's shape, production costs and visual language should be constantly compared with the role of the work in relation to its readership.[157] This leads us to amplification and activation — the acts that increase the reach of a particular work to their intended audience (amplification), and provide tools, resources or invitations for engagement (activation). In the current landscape of the contemporary photobook, activation is often a role that is outsourced to the readers. As interested individuals with specialist knowledge and a passion for the medium, they will not only be seeking and occupying spaces in which the book may be presented, but will willingly undertake the work required to engage with a publication once it is in front of them. In the future I call for, it is hoped that this may apply to a smaller number of works.

154
These groups clearly overlap (see 'Photobooks & community').

155
Distilled, the photographic book-photobook's use of the codex is as container, the artist's book-photobook as artwork and the photo essay-photobook as carrier (see 'Photobooks & intent').

156
This may seem an obvious point to make — that intent should inform production — but as the findings of this book have shown, there are times when discourse and post-digital production tendencies may derail or obfuscate this connection.

157
If a work is only seeking to speak with like-minded individuals with an interest in the photobook (thus operating in a small part of the artist's book-photobook lineage), makers may not need to engage this stage with the rigour of some other publications. Amani Willett spoke of this in referring to the difference in working toward *The Disappearance of Joseph Plummer* (2017), in which the process 'seemed more simple' than *A Parallel Road* (2020), which was complicated by a broader and more diverse audience.

Fig. 13

Intent
Production
Amplification
Activation
Reading
Photobook discourse

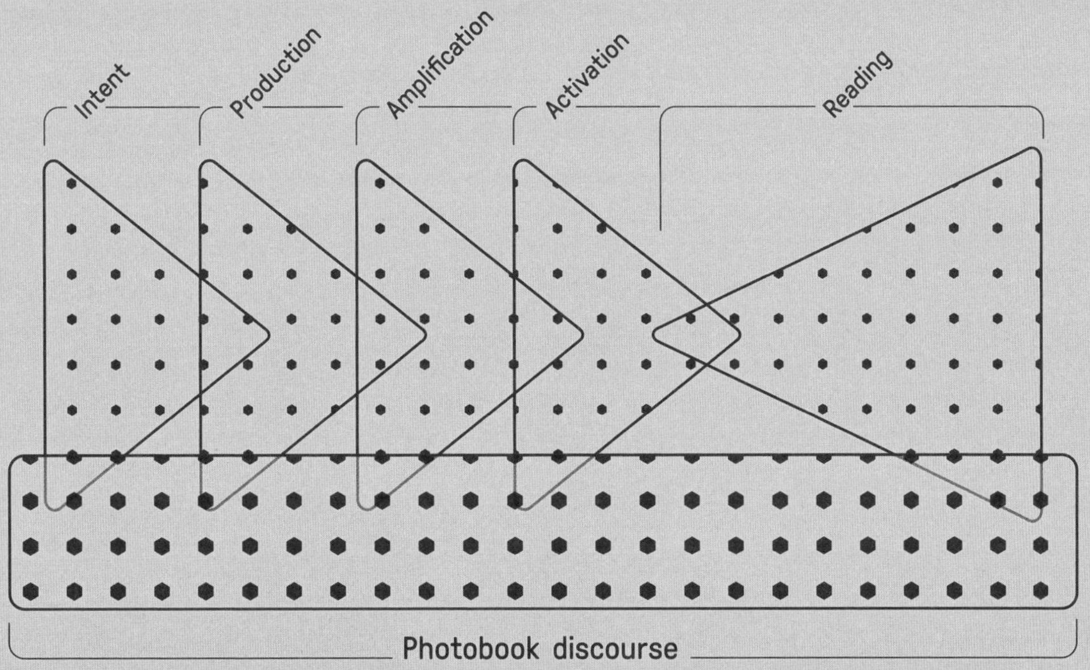

‘I truly believe that if you’ve been really honest with every single element of the book, and it’s been created over a period of time where you’ve questioned why you’re creating what you are, and why the form of what you’ve created exists in the way that it does, and you have reasons that you’re honest about, that do justice to the work, then they come through.’ (Anshika Varma)

If the framework is adopted in full, its amplification and activation stages will not pose significant problems, since the work will be in a form that is suited for these aspects of publishing. Often however, if a secondary audience is considered,[158] or if intent and production are not aligned closely, these latter stages will have to overcome additional barriers. Finally, the work is with the reader — a point that has been made possible through a series of conscious acts. At this stage, readers bring to the work their lived experience, taste, knowledge of subject and awareness of the medium — baggage that will be unique to each reader and informed by the intent and expectation of their reading. Though engagement with the book will be influenced by the context of reception (production, amplification and activation), I have inverted the direction of this stage so as to emphasise the considerable weight and importance of the reader as meaning-maker.

Alongside five stages, the framework also includes a horizontal bar which partially obscures the acts behind it — a representation of a journey between maker and reader that can, at each stage, be impacted by the predominant photobook discourse.[159] The dominance of this feature is intended to remind those working with the photobook how their actions and perceptions may connect more closely with the expectations and legitimisations of the medium, rather than the purpose of the work itself. Finally, I should make clear that this framework can also be approached from right to left. In this direction, it is the critic, reviewer or judge who is imagined. I propose that the way in which the photobook is appraised could benefit from a critical consideration of the way in which a work has realised the logistics of publishing with regards to what it sets out to do. This is not to say that such a consideration needs to be forensic, but that noting cost, availability, accompanying resources and activities would be worthwhile if there is a belief in the possibilities of our medium to communicate in a rich manner to extended audiences.

158
A secondary audience may well be a palatable suggestion for many makers in the photobook world — meaning that the work can still operate in our community, which recognises its various efforts and intricacies, but it can also have a life and purpose outside.

159
I refer to 'discourse' in its widest sense, to include conversations, publications, institutions, awards and so on.

↳ A common lexicon

To aid the practical application of the framework, I have produced a series of questions that may be asked at specific junctures in the longitudinal process of publishing. I do not align them with stages, to allow for the possibility that some stages could be amended, removed or reworked for a variety of purposes. They are written for the maker, critic and interested reader, and can be accompanied by the terms used through this book — lineage, amplification, activation, and the eight acts of reading that help to foreground a predominantly veiled experience and provide a common language for a reading economy.[160] Answers to these questions must be honest, in order that the pull of the photobook and its ecology do not sway makers from the purpose of publishing.[161]

160
In small and subtle ways I have sought to introduce these questions and reflections and their answers into reviews of photobooks I have written, and in conversations with makers working towards publication.

161
Or in Phillip Zimmermann's words, books do not become 'sheep dressed up in wolves clothes' (2016).

- What does the work seek to do in the world?
- Why is this work being published?
- Who would enjoy seeing this photobook?
- Who would benefit from seeing this photobook?
- Who needs to see this photobook?
- What form does the work take as a photobook?
- What papers, bindings and production flourishes are used?
- How much does it cost to make a photobook like this?
- How does that impact the cost of purchase or ability to donate?
- What knowledge does the photobook rely on?
- What contextual information or resources are presented with (or in) the photobook?
- How can the work be seen without purchase?
- Who knows about this photobook?
- Who is speaking about this photobook?
- What has happened to the work as a result of publishing?
- How can the success of this photobook be measured?

↳ Where responsibility lies

A potential tension in the framework I have presented, and in the proposition that we may consider a reading economy for the photobook, is that it could be said to dampen or dilute the artistic freedom that has been so pivotal in shaping the contemporary photobook. Partly, this is resolved in considerations of the intent of publishing (see 'Photobooks & intent'), but there remain questions about how (and how much) publications are adjusted for given audiences, and where responsibility for this, or subsequent readership-enhancing acts, lie.

Both Natasha Christia and Anshika Varma, who are strong proponents of the need to make the photobook accessible and bring it to a broader audience, are adamant in not infringing on the freedom of the artist and their desire to make their work as they see fit. This transfers a responsibility from the production of the publication to amplification and activation, and for Varma, towards initiatives like her own Offset Projects, which can be the 'bridge in the middle' of the maker and reader. In many instances I agree with this strategy, but I also believe that a reliance on stages beyond production — a leaning on amplification and activation — can reduce the possibilities of the book. For me, it is the makers, or more precisely, the photographer/artist, that must begin to take more responsibility for the role of their work in the world.[162] This role will be unique to each and every work, but there are three areas that, if addressed honestly, can be transformative for our medium: quality, placement and tiering.

162
Though I stress the location of this responsibility, I also maintain that there is space for a shift in the role and worth of publishers, who could become as renowned for their amplification tactics and activation strategies as their artistic realisations. Rather than photographers seeking the publisher with the best reputation for print, they might seek out those with the best connections to specific audiences or support for outreach initiatives and open-access iterations.

The first of these (quality), is a product of some of the discussions in 'Photobooks & access', as well as the landscape of 'Photobooks & the post-digital'. When I talk of an addressing of quality, I refer to the construction and printing of the book, and though this may mean removing or downplaying elements of production, it is only where such adjustments better serve expanded readerships. It may seem strange to desire a lessening of quality, but my position is that high-fidelity reproductions and intricate production techniques have become de facto in the photobook ecology, and that a certain element of snobbery around simpler printing and binding options is ultimately restrictive. It is the maker-centric nature of the photobook community (see 'Photobooks & community') that seeks the fine papers and inks that have little bearing on the work itself and its reception beyond those who are so connected with the medium. Significantly, here I am not suggesting a necessary simplification of design, but a questioning of the need for costly haptic touches.[163]

I come quickly to my next area for makers' consideration — *tiering*. In tiering I refer to two distinct elements of publication. The first is in the construction of the work itself, where several editions could allow for the ideal, or artist's, edition to fulfil the freedom of the maker (and demands of the photobook community and collectors), while another publication prioritises the amplification, activation and readership of the work away from its place as a niche and expensive work.[164] The second element of tiering is specifically aligned with activation by presenting companion text or resources that offer multiple ways in, and out, of a publication. They may be ignored or eschewed by some readers, but provide for librarians, educators and those new to the subject or medium, a variety of ways in which to engage with the work or construct learning around it.[165] While the former aspect of tiering, in which different editions or iterations are able to serve particular readerships is rare, the past few years have seen some resources emerge.[166]

Finally, the third area — placement. Perhaps the single most significant act of amplification that combats the legitimising tendencies of our photobook community is a rethinking of the places to which books are sent. Currently, many photographers set aside books to be

163
This area for consideration is of course ripe for application to out-of-print works. In 2014 I worked with Nathan Pearce on the book *Midwest Dirt*, which quickly sold out a limited run, shortly after Pearce made a 'bootleg edition' (2015) at his local copy shop, which was sold for a fraction of the cost of the original ($6).

164
The value of tiering is something seen by Ángel González at The Library Project, who in creating a friendly retail space in which members of the public feel comfortable browsing, considered different levels of engagement to be catered for. It is also possible to consider tiered access with a single publication: Laura El-Tantawy's pricing structure for *The People* (2015), meant that it was free for Egyptians and €25 for those outside the publication's subject nation.

165
A series of questions, a reading list, an idea for a small workshop, seminar or practical task. Lindsay Morris' *You are You* (2015a) is a good example, with a large reading list exploring gender creativity for parents, children and teens online (Morris 2015b).

166
Projects like 10x10 Photobooks' Insta Salons and MACK's *MACK LIVE* both offer insightful content to interested readers in the form of presentations, performances and Q&A, though both can be said to remain predominantly aligned with a photobook, or photography, ecology.

sent to platforms of photobook review, or respected individuals who publish the results online, but seldom are there links to places in which the book can be accessed without purchase, even when it is out of print and little damage can be done to market values. Few photobooks reside in town or village libraries, fewer still in schools and colleges not specialising in the arts.[167] This is a question of value and discourse: the value of photobooks to society beyond our ecology, and discourse in the sense that there is little existing interest or conversation around amplification and activation — a situation that decreases the chances of such acts occurring. There are many who may share Tiffany Jones' sentiment that making books into 'elite artworks' is limiting, and that having books in libraries 'to carry on stories for future generations' is far more important and exciting, but fewer who respond in action. Amak Mahmoodian, who has gained considerable accolades in the photobook and photography community, most recently winning the Arles Photo-Text award with *Zanjir* (2019), is clear on the role that libraries can play alongside arts institutions:

> 'I start with libraries because that's where I educated myself as a student and that's something that I won't forget and I want other students to have the same opportunity. So of course I also make the book for recognition by museums and I'm happy when Tate say they want a copy of all of my books. It's a great pleasure, but pretty much all university libraries have my book and if they ask, then I send it for free, because that's the place where we can educate people and share with people, especially when the stories are of resistance and identity.'

Coupled with placement itself is the promotion of placement and availability. Though the majority of makers will list a photobook's presence in a prestigious archive or photobook collection, few provide links to where the book can be seen or engaged with without

167
Sarah Bodman: 'If you're using social documentary to bring awareness to something, but only making 300 copies, how many copies would you need to change the world? Or is it 300 well-placed copies? If they all went to public libraries, then that's different from if they're going to 300 photobook collections ... you're preaching to the converted, or they might just think 'Oh, great photos' rather than 'Oh, now I know that'.

purchase.[168] Time is spent in announcing and linking to reviews, shortlists or winning accolades, so it would be fair to expect that this can simply be extended in remit. There are hundreds of alternative areas with which makers may choose to engage in seeking to realise a future for the photobook, and within them, thousands of options. Those outlined here should not be taken as prescribing action, but I hope, sparking thought.

Combined, the findings and suggestions of this book strive to support the progression of the contemporary photobook. They have emerged from interrogating the role of the reader, the purpose of publishing and the contemporary situation of the medium in the post-millennium, and have been formed by, and greatly benefited from, voices around the photobook ecology. Whilst my approach has been critical of the insularity of the contemporary photobook, my belief in the medium as one with great opportunity to create spaces of learning, sharing and connecting has not only remained constant, but has been solidified in this process. *Photobooks &* has sought to put into action my call for more thought regarding readers, and tactics by which to engage them — an exercise in amplification and activation of my PhD and the years of research that led to it. As such, it is not positioned as absolute, and I hope that readers will consider entering into a conversation with me and the work: I am excited at the prospect that there may be remixing, reworking and augmentation of what is found on these pages. For now, I return to the core tenet of this publication as a marker of my intent in its publishing:

> To facilitate a progression of the discourse around the contemporary photobook, to foreground purpose, publishing and a reading economy, and in doing so reconnect making, making public and critical discourse.

168
Video flick-throughs or presentations of photobooks are common, but they strip much of the communicative potential of the medium from the object itself. Reading is no longer dictated by the reader, tactile engagement is lost, and small details as well as text are not visible. Thus, these performances are trailers for a possible reading experience rather than a means of access.

‘What happens in our field now is that people expect automatic validation and recognition of their work. I have a feeling that in 100 years many of the names that are relevant today will be completely forgotten and there will be other works that will be praised. The real work takes place in a very silent way.’ (Natasha Christia)

Clearly one of the most significant resources for this chapter is Matthew Stadler's *The Ends of the Book: Reading, Economies and Publics* (2018), but it is worth investigating Publication Studio (which Stadler founded) in full, as well as specific titles like *Plastic Words* (Bailey 2015) and *Publication Studio Portable: A Mobile Publishing Manual* (Sully et al. 2019). In a similar vein, Temporary Services' *Publishing in the Realm of Plant Fibres and Electrons* (2014) may be beneficial. *Republishing: The Virtues of Retelling* edited by Virginie Bobin and Mathilde Villeneuve (2012) has played a significant part in the thought in this chapter. Then, since the library has been spoken of at several points, I might look to recommend *Meeting Grounds, Reader One: The Public Library*, edited by Amy Gowan (2020), Eva Olthof's *Return to Rightful Owner* (2015) and Anna-Sophie Springer and Etienne Turpin's *Fantasies of the Library* (2016).

In *Source* magazine's special photobook edition, three essays are presented regarding photobooks 'in the real world', with each taking a different photobook as its subject (Binns 2016)(Noble 2016)(Long 2016). While only one of these essays really starts to deal with the action of the photobook outside our own community (Noble's consideration of Stephen Ferry's *Violentologia*, 2012), they are nonetheless an interesting marker to consider the possibilities of the medium. Continuing this theme, I might highlight several interviews that I conducted in my research — they cover a wide range of topics, but my conversations with Sarah Bodman and Natasha Christia in particular explore both the status quo and possible futures for the contemporary medium (photobookclub.org/photobooks&).

Finally, in 2019 the International Summer School of Photography had a thematic residency titled *Photography and the World*, from which a publication available for download was made (ISSP 2019). Though it deals mostly with making visual work (and not its publication), it is still a rich resource, and with its opening line, 'Who is asking questions about photography and the world?', fits closely with much of the sentiment of this chapter.

Glossary

Activation — Acts that energise the book through spaces, events, workshops and other strategies that generate a readership rather than just an increased audience.

Amplification — A term borrowed from Michael Bhaskar, amplification refers to acts that result in the increased distribution and audience of a given work (2013, 114).

Artist's book — Much like with the photobook, there is little agreement on neat definitions of the artist's book. In this publication it refers to works that are primarily 'defined (and confined) by an art context' (Lippard, 1985:47). Artists' books may often use the form of the book as integral to the work itself and can feature a variety of visual media. Clive Phillpot's *Booktrek* (2013) offers a starting point for an expansive investigation into the nature of the artist's book.

Audience — The intended groups, communities or institutions with which the photobook maker seeks to engage through publication. The audience is not a single person encountering the book, but this individual (the reader), resides within the audience.

Author — Used in order to separate the author of the photographic work contained in a photobook and the other creatives who play an instrumental role in publishing, see also: Maker.

Dummy — The photobook dummy is a proof version of a photobook that has historically been used as a step towards publishing. The dummy has become a more public component of the photobook's life in fairs festivals and competitions in the post-millennium.

Graphical elicitation — A method of data collection and subsequent analysis that can be employed to assist the review of experience and emotion, complimenting 'data collected through the interviewing process' and 'stimulating thoughts' (Copeland and Agosta, 2012, 514).

Networked technology — This term defines a shift in technology from isolated to connected, and thus brings with it opportunities for email, message boards, forums, social media and web collaboration. The term is a more common way of speaking about the technologies that Jon Palfrey and Urs Gasser describe as 'linked-digital', which began in the late 1990s (2008).

Maker — The term maker is used to highlight the multiple people involved in the production and publishing of a photobook, to recognise that it is often not a singular individual's endeavour and instead may include: 'an author, an editor, a designer, a publisher, and a printer' (Schmid 2018).

Photobook — The photobook is a single or multi-authored, bound work with photography as its primary content. It is an expression of a unified thought, subject, position, location or time, which has been constructed with awareness of the physical book as output.

The Photobook Club — A project I founded in 2010 to promote and facilitate discussion around the photobook. The Photobook Club is a global community of readers.(photobookclub.org)

The photobook community — A group of individuals who coalesce around the contemporary photobook in fairs, festivals, blogs and social media spaces, as well as constructing the medium itself in book publishing.

The photobook ecology — A term borrowed from Daniel Boetker-Smith (2015, 24), used to refer to the community, events, discourse and products that construct and react to the photobook.

Post-digital — The post-digital refers to a comparative settling after the storm of digital. It speaks of the omnipresence of networked technology in our lives and how we have responded to it. The predominant application of the term derives from Florian Cramer's investigation into the post-digital first published in 2014.

Post-photography — A new landscape of photography that has seen a transformation from the fixed to fluid image, and with it a series of challenges to the ontological understanding of the medium.

Print-on-demand — A publishing method whereby copies of a publication are only produced when they are bought or requested individually or in multiples.

Publishing — The holistic process of making work public. It speaks of the many acts and pragmatics involved in realising and activating a publication. It involves the pricing, edition size, distribution, point of sale and promotion of the work, as well as a plethora of other components.

Reader — An imagined and actual audience member who spends time with a given photobook. When speaking of the reader, I also refer to readers, and the reading they perform.

Readership — A term used when speaking of the audience and their reading, combined.

Reading economy — A term used by Matthew Stadler (2018, 118-27) and that I expand in 'Photobooks & the future' to refer to a landscape in which the reader, and strategies of engaging with readers, become more prominent in the discourse and action of the photobook ecology.

Resources

This is not a complete list of resources that relate to the photobook, but rather a series of texts that help to locate the medium in broader conversations around publishing, photography and the arts. Alongside platforms that offer a view of the current photobook landscape I have sought to include works that have been pivotal in my own research and those that could route investigations towards new fields of study. Together, this resource list is a snapshot of the photobook ecology, and a myriad of possible points of departure for further investigation.

↳ Printed material

Artists' Books: A Critical Anthology and Sourcebook (Lyons 1985) — 15 essays on artists' books including Alex Sweetman's writing on the 'photo-bookwork', Ulises Carrión's *New Art of Making Books*, Lucy Lippard on the public artist's book and much more.

Books on Books on Artists' books (Desjardin 2013) — Arnaud Desjardin's bibliography of books, leaflets and catalogues, which charts the development of the artist's book discourse is an incredibly useful reference point for further research.

Booktrek (Phillpot 2013) — A great resource for those interested in the history of the artist's book in the US and Europe in particular. Phillpot's essays in this collection begin in 1972 and include several key attempts to define and contextualise the medium and its spectrum of different forms and styles of outputs.

Code-X, Paper, Ink, Pixel and Screen (Aldred & Waeckerlé 2015) — Edited by Danny Aldred and Emmanuelle Waeckerlé, this is a publication that interrogates the 'shifting sands' of publishing after and through the digital. Andrew Lister's interview with Hans Gremmen and Delphine Bedel's writing about *Meta/Books* in particular are worth seeking out. I have my own chapter in this publication too, which frames *The Photobook Club* in response to hierarchical conversations.

Dynamics of the Photobook Market (Jones 2019) — Tiffany Jones' MA thesis, since published as a small book under her imprint *Overlapse Books*, is a great resource for those researching the photobook market, which I might suggest will be anyone in the process of making, or selling, photobooks.

Fantasies of the Library (Springer & Turpin 2016) — A book that, in its collection of works, reconsiders what a library is, and what it can be. Readers interested in this area may also wish to look at Amy Gowen's *Meeting Grounds Reader One: The Public Library* (2020).

How we See: Photobooks by Women (Lederman et al. 2019) — From 10x10 Photobooks, this publication challenges the white-male-constructed canon of photobooks and presents a number of influential photobooks by women. It is to be joined soon by *What They Saw: Historical Photobooks by Women, 1843–1999.*

Imprint: Visual Narratives in Books and Beyond (Badger 2013) — A collection of essays on the photobook from various perspectives, this publication brings a good deal of depth to reflections on the medium. Though it is not indicated in the title, this book is photobook-centric.

Making Things Public (Latour & Weibel 2005) — Bruno Latour's introductory section alone in this hard-to-source book is worth seeking out for those interested in the potential for buildings, objects — and thus books — to act as temporary spaces of political conversation.

Photobibliomania — An exhibition and resulting publication (fold-out poster), this project from David Solo and the ICP Library in New York provides a list of books on photobooks up to its publication in 2014. So, while there have been many new titles since, it is a good resource for the numerous works that canonised the photobook (globally and locally).

Photographic Books (McCausland 1942) — This is only a single essay by Elisabeth McCausland, which featured in issue 43 of The Complete Photographer, but is the first known writing on photography and the book and thus also the first use of the term *photographic book*. Though much of her work has been digitised by the Archives of American Art, this article has not, and is hard to come by.

Photography and the Artist's Book (Wilkie et al. 2012) — Some interesting essays from around the time when the photobook is becoming a topic of conversation in academia. There are some useful thoughts on definition and location for those exploring that area, as well as reflections on historical and contemporary publishing practices.

Post-digital Print: The Mutation of Publishing since 1894 (Ludovico 2012) — An instrumental publication in my own research, Alessandro Ludovico's book dissects the history of publishing and its engagement with electronics in an accessible and vibrant manner. A rich asset in our understanding of the contemporary landscape of publishing.

Publish your Photography Book (Himes and Swanson 2014) — In content this book is heavily maker-centric, but it includes a thorough appendix of resources (many specific to the photobook) regarding distribution, bookshops, blogs, awards and so on.

Publishing as Artistic Practice (Gilbert 2016) — Edited by Annette Gilbert, this publication features a range of texts exploring publishing in a broad manner — from libraries and the social life of the book to materiality and aesthetics.

Scenes in a Library: Reading the Photograph in the Book, 1843–1875 (Armstrong 1998) — With a focus on British books, Carol Armstrong considers the period in which the photographic image became increasingly reliant and embedded with the page. Though strictly historical, there is much to be said for a greater comprehension of how this period has helped shape the way we think of the photobook today.

Talking the Boundless Book: Art, Language & the Book Arts (Higgins et al. 1995) — Essays from the Minnesota Center for Book Arts Symposium, this collection covers hermeneutics, economics of small press publishing, what the book is, and early electronic texts.

The Blue Notebook: Journal for Artists' books — Edited by the team at the Centre for Fine Print Research at the University of the West of England, who also produce the *Artist's Book Yearbook* and have number of sources available online. (bookarts.uwe.ac.uk/blue-notebook)

The Book is A—live! (Waeckerlé & Sawdon-Smith 2013) — A publication emerging from the BOOKLIVE! Symposium held in 2012, this is a rich resource for exploring innovation and thought in contemporary publishing (not specifically the photobook or artist's book). Contributors include Arnaud Desjardin, Joan Fontcuberta, Paul Soulellis, Sharon Helgason Gallagher and Sarah Bodman.

The Book: On Endless Possibilities (Christia 2015) — Natasha Christia's publication offers a wealth of insights that are open and critical. The conversation between Ramon Pez, Laia Abril and Gonzalo Golpe is particularly illuminating.

The Century of Artists' Books (Drucker 2004) — Considered to be one of the most significant pieces of work to help historicise and contextualise the artist's book.

The Content Machine (Bhaskar 2013) — Michael Bhaskar's theory of publishing features in 'Photobooks & access' in this publication. His writing, which looks at all forms of publishing, is accessible and straightforward. It is a useful companion for anyone embarking on the journey of making work public.

The Form of the Book Book (Smet et al. 2010) — Essays on design, reading and the possible futures of the book. This publication is not photobook-specific, nor is it focused on the artist's book in particular, though the visual book in all its guises is prominent.

The Journal of Artists' Books — Though this journal was discontinued in 2020, some university libraries may have copies, and some sections have been digitised. (journalofartistsbooks.org)

The Photobook Review — An indispensable resource, Aperture's *Photobook Review* is a newspaper journal available to subscribers of Aperture (with a number of articles available for free online). *The Photobook Review* features a range of voices and a rare depth of engagement with the photobook. (aperture.org/pbr)

Structure of the Visual Book (Smith 1994) — Keith Smith's book on bookmaking does much more than consider the physical structure of the codex, including providing a succinct account of how meaning can be constructed in sequences of pages.

Various Small Books: Referencing Various Small Books by Ed Ruscha (Brouws et al. 2013) — This volume features a range of book homages to Ed Ruscha's publications, as well as essays on the artist's impact on the field.

What We See When We Read: A Phenomenology (Mendelsund 2014) — Peter Mendelsund's beautifully illustrated book looks at how we construct mental images from non-visual books that we read. It is a fascinating introduction to the phenomenology of reading.

Writing Machines (Hayles 2002) — Katherine Hayles explores the transition of text to hypertext and in doing so calls for 'medium-specific' critique. The transitions with which the book deals offer a series of parallels with the photobook in the post-digital and post-photographic era.

YET magazine: What We Learned About Publishing (2020) — There are a number of magazines that have had a special issue dedicated to the photobook, and all are worth seeking out (*Source* 2016, *Foam* 2013, *The British Journal of Photography* 2015, *Photofile* 2015, *PDN* 2013), but this 2020 *YET* special issue is particularly useful. It is an insightful reflection on current photobook discourse and involves a variety of names that can lead to further research. (yet-magazine.com)

↳ Online Resources

2021 Contemporary Artists' Book conference — Due to the pandemic, this annual conference went online in 2021 and has been made available on the Printed Matter Youtube channel. This year's conference focused on the role of criticism but brought other topics in too. There is much to explore, but highlights include the conversation between Anshika Varma and Dyanita Singh and the opening sessions with Aaron Cohick, Johanna Drucker, Megan N. Liberty, Levi Sherman, Corina Reynolds, David Solo and Vivian Sming. (bit.ly/CABC_2021)

5b4 Photography and Books — Jeffrey Ladd, formerly of *Errata Editions* runs this Patreon blog with articles on some well-known, and other much less-well-known photobooks. (patreon.com/jeffrey_ladd)

A Manifesto for the Book — Edited by Tom Sowden and Sarah Bodman of the Centre for Fine Print Research, this is a free PDF that includes a range of interviews, essays and other musings on the artist's book. (bookarts.uwe.ac.uk/manifesto-for-the-book/)

A Peer Reviewed Journal About: Post-digital Research — This open-access journal issue focuses on the post-digital and has some really useful texts — in particular, Florian Cramer's summary presented in *What is the Post-digital?* and Lotte Philipsen's *Who's Afraid of the Audience?* (aprja.net)

Africa in the Photobook — Ben Krewinkel (author of *Conversations with Gualbert*) has been exploring 'the changing visual representation of Africa as expressed through the medium of the photobook' in books by African photographers, those made in Africa, and books made outside by non-African photographers and writers. The project is due to be developed into a set of publications. (africainthe-photobook.com)

Asia Pacific Photobook Archive — Daniel-Boetker Smith launched this project in 2013 and now runs it alongside Isabella Capezio. The website offers an online archive of the books in the collection and information on festivals in the Asia Pacific area, as well as when the archive travels. (photobookarchive.com)

Belphotobooks — The Belgian Photobooks blog run by Stefan Vanthuyne may be sporadic in posts but features some great pieces that operate with some depth regarding the contemporary photobook. Natasha Christia's writing on the potentiality of the photobook, and a three-part interview with Stanley Wolukau-Wanambwa are particularly illuminating. (belphotobooks.org)

C4 Journal — A space that has been set up in order to explore and promote work that is 'often sidelined in more mainstream discussion and debate'. Primarily C4 Journal looks at photography in the book form, via contextual and critical short essays, as well as interviews. (c4journal.com)

Book Art Theory blog — A fantastic resource from the College Book Arts Association with regular contributions and discussions. Posts are easy to digest and often link to further reading on the subject. Book arts in its broadest sense is under consideration here, with the photobook featuring on occasion. Though it has not been updated for some time, an extensive list of texts on artists' books can be found in the 'resources' section. (collegebookart.org/bookarttheory)

Digital Archive of Artists' Publishing — This is an exciting project from Ami Clarke of Banner Repeater and Arnaud Desjardin. The initiative seeks to provide access initially to the 1,000+ strong archive at the Hackney Downs train station, before expanding from there, and is to be one of the most substantial online archives of artists' books available. (daap.network)

Gabriela Cendoya — This eponymous blog shares Cendoya's love of photobooks and love of sharing them. The content has certainly slowed down, but it's still a good visit, especially to check the pulse of the Spanish photobook scene. (gabrielacendoya.wordpress.com)

Market? What Market? — A publication conceived and realised by Daria Tuminas and Moritz Neumüller, *Market? What Market?* coincided with the 2017 edition of the Unseen photobook fair. A range of voices discuss the photobook community and audience with interesting conversations on pragmatics and distribution. (bit.ly/market_what_market)

PHOTO / BOOK / CLUB: Connections Made and Missed, Digital and Other, Between the Contemporary Photobook and its Readers — My own PhD thesis which can be accessed using the British Library's *Ethos* service. *PHOTO / BOOK / CLUB* will provide some additional data and reflections not in this publication, in particular around the process of reading and application of lineages in publishing.

Photobook Journal — This website features regular introductions to newly published work, as well as resources for the photobook community — competitions, awards, festivals, publishers and so on. (photobookjournal.com)

Photo-eye blog — This active blog platform from Photo-eye (booksellers) includes many reviews, occasional interviews and the annual best-of lists, which have featured an increasingly broad range of voices since 2015 (all are still available to see). (blog.photo-eye.com)

The Digital Photobook — Though now discontinued (2013), Martin Brink's blog provides a useful archive of experimentations with the digital photobook. PDFs, iBooks, apps and proprietary formats are all included here, as well as some interesting physical/digital comparisons. (thedigitalphotobook.blogspot.com)

The Indie Photobook Library — Now a closed collection found at the Beinecke rare book library at Yale, the online archive of works is still available and features over 2,000 publications. (indiephotobooklibrary.org)

The Many Faces of the Photobook: Establishing the Origins of Photobookwork Practice — José Luis Neves' PhD thesis, which looks at the origins of what he refers to as the 'photobookwork', will be of particular interest to those exploring the photobook before the millennium. It is available via the British Library's *Ethos* service. (bit.ly/neves_photobook_thesis)

The Post-digital Publishing Archive — The aim of the P-DPA is to 'systematically collect, organise and keep trace of experiences in the fields of art and design that explore the relationships between publishing and digital technology.' (p-dpa.net)

↳ Multi-platform projects

10x10 Photobooks — A multi-platform non-profit advancing knowledge of the new and old in photobooks. 10x10's publications, reading rooms, grants and salons are important and influential interventions in the photobook landscape. Its website is the first place to head, and if you don't live in New York or have access to their publications, there's still much to engage with in their Insta Salons. (10x10photobooks.org)

Asia Art Archive's *Mobile Library* — The Mobile Library from AAA has popped up in Nepal, Myanmar, Sri Lanka and Vietnam, each time with a set of outreach activities in public programming to help activate the collection. (aaa.org.hk/en/programmes/programmes/mobile-library)

Hydra — A multi-platform photography institution in Mexico, Hydra considers the photobook as a core element of what it does — with a bookstore, library, publishing arm and bookmaking workshops. (hydra.lat)

Offset Projects — Offset Projects, based in New Delhi and run by Anshika Varma, aims to create 'channels of engagement' with photography and book-making via talks, workshops, residencies and a travelling pop-up library. The *guftgu* series of talks, which went online in the pandemic and is available on the Offset Projects Youtube page, is accessible to all and very valuable. (offsetprojects.in)

Reminders Photography Stronghold — An initiative based in Tokyo with multiple tranches, including workshops, a library and gallery space. Publishing is very much central to Yumi Goto and her colleagues' projects with the platform. (reminders-project.org)

Self Publish, Be Happy — Founded by Bruno Ceschel, whose voice has come to be central to the contemporary photobook discourse, this project comprises a collection, publishing arm, outreach activities, educational projects and has played a big role in *Offprint London* programming as well as devising the *photobook:RESET* event in 2018.

The bookRoom — A post-digital research and publishing platform in the School of Fine Art and Photography at the University for the Creative Arts, led by Emmanuelle Waeckerlé. bookRoom has tracked the impact of digital technology on printed material and their use, and the parallel histories and practices of the artist's book and the photobook. Conferences, publications and research subjects can be found via the website.
(thebookroom.net)

The Photobook Museum — A diverse initiative dedicated to education and the photobook. Of particular interest may be the publication *The Photobook in Art and Society*, which was a collaboration between the Photobook Museum and the Montag Stiftung Kunst und Gesellschaft and features writing on the experimentations undertaken in bringing the photobook to a broader public, as well as wider texts on the photobook today.
(thephotobookmuseum.com)

Interviews

The conversations I have had with a variety of voices from the photobook ecology have been instrumental in the formation of my research and this publication. Though in these pages only short extracts of the full interviews are presented, transcriptions of many interviews are available online at photobookclub.org/photobooks&. A full list of the individuals featured in this book are presented here, with a brief note on their affiliation with organisations, initiatives or publications.

Alejandro Acin — Artist, designer and educator. Director of IC Visual Lab

Eman Ali — Artist and author of the photobook Succession (2019)

Mathieu Asselin — Artist and investigative documentary photographer. Author of Monsanto©: A Photographic Investigation (2017)

Sarah Bodman — Senior Research Fellow for Artists' Books at the Centre for Fine Print Research (CFPR) and editor of The Book Arts newsletter

Bruno Ceschel — Writer, curator, publisher and educator. Founder of Self Publish, Be Happy

Natasha Christia — Curator, writer and educator. Author of *The Book: On Endless Possibilities* (2015)

Juan Cires — Artist. Co-founder and organiser of the Photobook Club Madrid.

Ángel Luis González — Founder of The Library Project and director of PhotoIreland.

Larissa Leclair — Writer and curator. Founder of The Indie Photobook Library

Russet Lederman, Dolly Meieran and Olga Yatskevich — The team behind 10x10 Photobooks' publications, reading rooms, salons and research projects

Michael Mack — Publisher, MACK books

Amak Mahmoodian — Artist and educator. Author of *Shenasnameh* (2016) and *Zanjir* (2019)

Lesley Martin — Creative director of Aperture Foundation, editor and publisher of *The Photobook Review*

Tate Shaw — Artist, writer and educator. Director of the Visual Studies Workshop

Doug Spowart — Artist, writer and independent photobook researcher

Jon Uriarte — Curator of digital programs at the Photographers Gallery. Founder and former organiser of the Photobook Club Barcelona

Anshika Varma — Curator and photographer. Founder of Offset Projects

Amani Willett and Tiffany Jones — Photographer (Willett) and publisher (Jones – Overlapse books) of *The Disappearance of Joseph Plummer* and *A Parallel Road*

References

Abenavoli, Valentina. 2019. 'Swaying Time on a Flatland.' In *How We See: Photobooks by Women*, by Russet Lederman, Olga Yatskevich, and Michael Lang, 25–29. New York: 10x10 Photobooks.

Abril, Laia. 2014. *The Epilogue*. Stockport: Dewi Lewis.

Abril, Laia., Ramon Pez, and G Golpe. 2015. 'Let's Kill the Ego.' In *The Book: On Endless Possibilities: Independent Publishing Fair, Barcelona 2015, edited by Natasha Christia*, 24-31. Barcelona: The Folio Club.

Aldred, Danny, and Emmanuelle Waeckerlé, eds. 2015. Code-X: *Paper, Ink, Pixel and Screen*. Farnham: bookRoom press.

Ali, Eman. 2019. *Succession*. n.p. Eman Ali.

Andrews, Blake. n.d. 'Book of the Week: Selected by Blake Andrews.' Photo-eye (blog), Accessed 14 May 2021.https://blog.photoeye.com/2020/11/book-of-week-selected-by-blake-andrews_23.html.

Aperture. 2021. 'Paris Photo/ Aperture Foundation PhotoBook Awards Entry.' Accessed June 1, 2021, https://aperture.org/calls-for-entry/photobook-awards/.

Archey, Karen, and Robin Peckham. 2014. *Art Post-Internet*. Beijing: Ullens Center for Contemporary Art, https://bit.ly/36BPacf.

Asselin, Mathieu. 2017. Monsanto®: *A Photographic Investigation*. Dortmund: Verlag Kettler.

Atkins, Anna. 1843. *Photographs of British Algae* : Cyanotype Impressions. London: Anna Atkins.

Ault, Julie. 2006. 'Interview with Lucy R. Lippard on Printed Matter.' December 2006, https://www.printed-matter.org/tables/41.

Badger, Gerry, and Martin Parr. 2004. *The Photobook: A History Volume I*. London: Phaidon.

———. 2006. *The Photobook: A History Volume II*. London: Phaidon.

———. 2014. *The Photobook: A History Volume III*. London: Phaidon.

Bailey, Louisa. 2015. *Plastic Words*. London: Publication Studio London

Bajohr, Hannes. 2016. 'Experimental Writing in Its Moment of Digital Technization: Post-Digital Literature and Print-on-Demand Publishing.' In *Publishing as Artistic*

Practice, edited by Annette Gilbert, 100–117. Berlin: Sternberg Press.

Bakker, Taco Hidde. 2012. 'Photobook Listmania.' *Taco Hidde Bakker* (blog). December 7, 2012, http://tacohiddebakker.com/blog/photobook-listmania/.

Barthes, Roland. 1977. *Image, Music, Text*. 5th ed. New York: Hill and Wang.

Bassett, Caroline. 2015. 'Not Now? Feminism, Technology, Postdigital.' In *Postdigital Aesthetics: Art, Computation and Design*, edited by David M. Berry and Michael Dieter, 136–50. London: Palgrave.

Bate, David. 2013. 'The Digital Condition of Photography: Cameras, Computers and Display.' In *The Photographic Image in Digital Culture*, edited by Martin Lister. 2nd ed, 77–94. London ; New York: Routledge, Taylor & Francis Group.

———. 2014. 'The Syntax of a Photowork.' In *Imprint; Visual Narratives in Books and Beyond*, edited by Hans Hedberg, Gunilla Knape, Tyrone Martnisson, and Louise Wolthers, 49–82. Stockholm: Art and Theory.

Baudrillard, Jean. 2005. *The System of Objects (Radical Thinkers)*. London: Verso Books.

Bénitah, Carolle. 2019. *Jamais Je Ne t'oublierai*. Bentivoglio: L'Artiere Editions.

Bennett, Andrew, and Nicholas Royle. 2009. *An Introduction to Literature, Criticism and Theory*. 4th ed. Harlow: Pearson.

Berry, David M., and Michael Dieter. 2015. *Postdigital Aesthetics: Art, Computation and Design*. London: Palgrave Macmillan.

Bey, Dawoud. 2018. *Dawoud Bey: Seeing Deeply*. Austin: University of Texas Press.

Bhaskar, Michael. 2013. *The Content Machine: Towards a Theory of Publishing from the Printing Press to the Digital Network*. London ; New York: Anthem Press.

Bicher, Anne-Katrin. 2020. 'From Concept to Realisation.' In *The Photobook in Art and Society: Participative Potentials of a Medium*, 151–98. Berlin; Cologne: Jovis; The PhotoBook Museum.

Binns, Rebecca. 2016. 'Photobooks in the Real World: Animals and Us.' *Source Photographic Review*, winter 2016, issue 88.

Bobin, Virginie, and Mathilde Villeneuve. 2012. 'Republishing: The Virtues of Retelling'. In *Republications*, edited by Virginie Bobin and Mathilde Villeneuve, 16–34. Berlin: Archive Books.

Boellstorff, Tom, Bonnie Nardi, Celia Pearce, and T. L. Taylor. 2012. *Ethnography and Virtual Worlds : A Handbook of Method*. Edited by Tom Boellstorff. Princeton: Princeton University Press.

Boetker-Smith, Daniel. 2015. 'An Interview with Michael Mack.' *Photofile*, spring/summer 2015, volume 97.

Borda, Silvia Grace. 2012. 'The Artist's Photographic Book: Towards a Definition.' In *Photography and the Artist's Book*, 28–61. Edinburgh: MuseumsEtc.

Bourdieu, Pierre. 1996. *Photography: A Middle-Brow Art*. Cambridge: Polity Press.

Bourke-White, Margaret, and Erskine Caldwell. 1937. *You Have Seen Their Faces*. New York: Viking Press.

Bush, Lewis. 2016. 'The Photo Book World: A Cult Not a Ghetto'. *Disphotic* (blog). February 15, 2016, http://www.disphotic.com/the-photo-book-world-a-cult-not-a-ghetto/.

Cairns, Antony, and Simon Baker. 2019. CTY. London: Morel Books.

Campany, David. 2014. "What's in a Name?' *The Photobook Review*, fall 2014, volume 7.

Capote, Truman, and Richard Avedon. 1959. *Observations*. New York: Simon and Schuster.

Carrión, Ulises. 1985. 'The New Art of Making Books'. In *Artists' Books : A Critical Anthology and Sourcebook*, 31–44. Rochester: Visual Studies Workshop Press.

Cascone, Kim. 2000. 'The Aesthetics of Failure: 'Post-Digital' Tendencies in Contemporary Computer Music.' *Computer Music Journal* 24 no.4: 12–18.

CCCB, Moritz Neumüller, and Fundació Foto Colectania, eds. 2017. *Photobook Phenomenon*. Barcelona: RM.

Cella, Bernhard, Leo Findeisen, and Agnes Blaha, eds. 2015. NO-ISBN: *On Self-publishing*. Cologne: Verlag der Buchhandlung Walther König.

Center for Book Arts. 2021. 'Book Art Review: Manifesto for New Book Art Criticism.' *Center for Book Arts* (blog). Accessed May 11, 2021. https://centerforbookarts.org/bar.

Ceschel, Bruno. 2015. *Self Publish, Be Happy: A DIY Photobook Manual and Manifesto*. New York: Aperture.

Chachra, Debbie. 2015. 'Why I Am Not a Maker.' *The Atlantic*. January 23, 2015, https://www.theatlantic.com/technology/archive/2015/01/why-i-am-not-a-maker/384767/.

Chandoha, Walter, Brittany Hudak and David La Spina. 2015. *Walter Chandoha: The Cat Photographer*. New York: Aperture.

Chao, Jade. 2019. 'Visual Storytelling and Independent Publishing: An Interview with Yumi Goto and Magnum Photos.' March 29, 2019, https://www.magnumphotos.com/theory-and-practice/visual-storytelling-independent-publishing-interview-yumi-goto/.

Chaplin, Lewis, and Sarah Piegay Espenon. 2021. 'Keynote Presentation: Lewis Chaplin and Sarah Piegay Espenon (Loose Joints).' Speech, London: May 20, 2021.

Christia, Natasha. 2020. 'The (Photo)Book: On Potentiality.' *Belgian Photobooks* (blog). August 19, 2020, https://belphotobooks.org/the-photobook-on-potentiality/.

Colberg, Jörg. 2011. 'Photography Is Over.' July 27, 2011. Video, 1:51, https://www.youtube.com/watch?v=Xd-ZC0bXSWA.

———. 2017. *Understanding Photobooks: The Form and Content of the Photographic Book*. New York: Routledge.

———. 2018. 'Towards a Photobook Taxonomy.' *Conscientious Photo- graphy Magazine* (blog). February 26, 2018, https://cphmag.com/photobook- taxonomy/.

Cole, Teju. 2020. *Fernweh*. London: MACK.

Cook, Guy. 1995. *Discourse and Literature: The Interplay of Form and Mind. Oxford*: Oxford University. Press.

Cooper, V. 2019. 'Liminal Moments at the Edges: Reading Montage Narratives in Artist's Books.' In *Artist's Book Yearbook, 2018–2019*, edited by Sarah Bodman, 14–23. Bristol: Impact Press.

Crager, Jack. 2014. 'Welcome to the Golden Age of DIY Photo Books.' Accessed November 14, 2016, http://www.americanphotomag.com/welcome-golden-age-diy-photo-books.

Cramer, Florian. 2014. 'What Is 'Post-Digital'?' *A Peer Reviewed Journal About*. 3 no.1 http://www.aprja.net/?p=1318.

Cresswell, J, and O Whitehead. 2015.'The Photobook: Some Thoughts.' *Loose Associations*, 2015, volume 1.

Curtis, Matthew, and Orlando Gili. 2021. *An Opinionated Guide to London Pubs*. London: Hoxton Mini Press

Cutts, Simon. 2007. *Some Forms of Availability: Critical Passages on the Book and Publication*. Cromford: Research Group for Artists Publishing.

Daly, Tim. 2018. 'Book Handling as a Research Method.' *The Blue Notebook: Journal for Artist's Books* 12 no.2: 54–61.

Dan, Nguyen Manh, and Nguyen Ngoc Hanh. 1969. *Viet Nam in Flames*. Saigon: The General Political Warfare Department of the Republic of Vietnam.

Dayanita Singh. 2019. *Dayanita Singh Zakir Hussain Maquette*. Göttingen: Steidl.

De Agostinis, Giada. 2017. 'Interview – Ben Krewinkel: Africa in the Photobook.' *Paper Journal*, October 4, 2017, https://paper-journal.com/africa-in-the-photobook-ben-krewinkel/.

Dean, Jodi. 2009. *Democracy and Other Neoliberal Fantasies; Communicative Capitalism and Other Left Politics*. Durham: Duke University Press.

Degiorgis, Nicolò. 2014. *Hidden Islam*. Bolzano: Rorhof.

———. 2014. *Hidden Islam: 479 Comments*. Bolzano: Rorhof.

Denderen, Ad van. 2003. *Go No Go: Les Frontières de L'Europe*. Arles: Actes Sud.

Drucker, Johanna. 2004. *The Century of Artists' Books*. New Edition, 2004. New York City: Granary Books.

Dugan, Thomas. 1979. *Photography Between Covers: Interviews with Photo-Bookmakers*. Rochester: Light Impressions.

Dworkin, Craig Douglas, Simon Morris, and Nick Thurston. 2012. *Do or DIY*. York: Information as Material.

Eagleton, Terry. 1994. *Literary Theory: An Introduction*. Oxford: Blackwell.

Edmaier, Bernhard. 2007. *Patterns of the Earth*. London: Phaidon.

El-Tantawy, Laura. 2015. بعشلا (*The People*). Cairo: Laura El-Tantawy.

Estrin, James. 2012. 'In an Age of Likes, Commonplace Images Prevail.' *New York Times Lens Blog* (blog). September 7, 2012, http://lens.blogs.nytimes.com/2012/09/07/in-an-age-of-likes-commonplace-images-prevail/?_r=0.

Fernández, H, ed. 1999. *Fotografía Pública: Photography in Print, 1919–1939*. Madrid: Museo Nacional Centro de Arte Reina Sofía.

Fernández, Horacio. 2011. 'Introduction.' In *The Latin American Photobook*, edited by Horacio Fernández, 9–28. New York: Aperture.

'Feting the Photobook'. 2014. *The Photobook Review*, fall 2014, volume 7.

FlakPhoto Books. 2019. 'About. Facebook. Accessed September 6, 2019, https://www.facebook.com/groups/flakphotobooks/about/.

Fletcher, Harrell. 2006. *The American War*. Atlanta: J & L Books.

Fontcuberta, Joan. 2015. *The Post-Photographic Condition*. Berlin: Kerber Verlag.

Foto8. 2010. 'Beyond Perceivable Benefits: Jonathan Worth's Experiment.' *FOTO8* (blog). January 28, 2010, https://www.foto8.com/live/beyond- perceivable-benefits-jonathan-worths- creative-commons-license-experiment/.

Fotobook Festival. 2015. 'Terms and Conditions for the Dummy Award 2015.' Accessed February 23, 2015, http://fotobookfestival.org/terms-conditions-shop/#ecen.

Friebe, Daniel, and Pete Goding. 2011. *Mountain High: Europe's 50 Greatest Cycle Climbs*. London: Quercus.

Galjaard, David. 2012. *Concresco*. n.p. David Galjaard.

Gauntlett, David. 2018. *Making Is Connecting: The Social Power of Creativity, from Craft and Knitting to Digital Everything*. 2nd ed. Cambridge: Polity.

Geismar, Haidy. 2015. 'Post-Photographic Presences, or How to Wear a Digital Cloak.' Photographies 8 no.3: 305–21. https://doi.org/10.1080/17540763.2015.1102760.

Gilberger, Ruth. 2020. 'Together We Are More.' In *The Photobook in Art and Society: Participative Potentials of a Medium*, 27–30. Berlin; Cologne: Jovis ; The PhotoBook Museum.

Gilbert, Annette, ed. 2016. *Publishing as Artistic Practice*. Berlin: Sternberg Press.

Goldin, Nan. 1986. The Ballad of Sexual Dependency. New York: Aperture.

Goldsmith, Kenneth. 2011. *Uncreative Writing: Managing Language in the Digital Age*. New York: Columbia University Press.

Gonzalez, Andres. 2019. *American Origami*. Amsterdam: Fw: Amsterdam.

Gowen, Amy, ed. 2020. *Meeting Grounds Reader One* – The Public Library. Eindhoven: Onomatopee.

Hagner, Michael. 2020. 'Hyperpresence and Reflection.' In *The Photobook in Art and Society: Participative Potentials of a Medium*,

407–12. Berlin; Cologne: Jovis ; The PhotoBook Museum.

Halpern, Greg. 2011. *A*. Atlanta: J & L Books.

Hamaya, Hiroshi. 1956. *Snow Land*. Tokyo: Mainichi Newspapers.

Hampton, Michael. 2015. *Unshelf-marked: Reconceiving the Artist's Book*. Devon: Uniform Books.

Heyman, Abigail. 1974. *Growing up Female: A Personal Photojournal*. New York: Holt, Rinehart and Winston.

Higginbottom, Richard, and Jack Greenwood. 2018. *On Hold*, publishing performance, Village Books, Leeds, Novemver 15, 2018.

Higgins, Dick. 1985. 'A Preface.' In *Artists' Books : A Critical Anthology and Sourcebook*, edited by Joan Lyons, 11–26. Rochester: Visual Studies Workshop Press.

Himes, Darius, and Mary Virginia Swanson. 2010. *Publish Your Photography Book*. New York: Princeton Architectural Press.

Homma, Takashi. 2014. *RRREECCONNSTRUCCTTT*. Tokyo: Goliga.

Huck, Alan. 2019. *I Walk toward the Sun Which Is Always Going Down*. London: MACK.

ICP Library, and D Solo. 2014. *Photobibliomania*. New York: Library of the International Center of Photography.

ISSP. 2019. *Photography and the World*. Riga: ISSP.

Jackson, Alecia Youngblood, and Lisa Mazzei. 2011. *Thinking with Theory in Qualitative Research : Viewing Data Across Multiple Perspectives*. London: Routledge.

Jobey, Liz. 2015. 'Why Photobooks Are Booming in a Digital Age.' *Financial Times*, February 27, 2015, https://www.ft.com/content/be1fd978-bceb-11e4-a917-00144feab7de.

Johnston, Matt, and Ken Schles. 2012. *Invisible City: A Digital Resource*. Coventry: The Photobook Club.

Jones, Tiffany. 2019. *Dynamics of the Photobook Market*. London: Overlapse.

Jude, Ron. 2020. *12 Hz*. London: MACK.

Jurgenson, Nathan. 2012. 'The IRL Fetish.' *The New Inquiry* (blog). June 28 2012, https://thenewinquiry.com/the-irl-fetish/.

Kelly, Kevin. 2008. 'Better Than Free.' *The Technium* (blog). January 31, 2008, http://kk.org/thetechnium/better-than-fre/.

Kessels, Erik. 2011. *24 Hrs In Photos*. Photography and sculpture. Foam, Amsterdam, 2012, http://www.kesselskramer.com/exhibitions/24-hrs-of-photos.

Kholeif, Omar, ed. 2014. *You Are Here: Art after the Internet*. Manchester: Cornerhouse.

Kitano, Takeshi. 2005. 'Takeshi Kitano Joue Avec 'Les Cahiers'.' *Les Cahiers Du Cinéma*, April 5, 2005, https://www.lemonde.fr/cinema/article/2005/04/05/takeshi-kitano-joue-avec-les-cahiers_635542_3476.html.

Kozinets, Robert V. 2010. *Netnography: Ethnographic Research in the Age of the Internet*. Thousand Oaks: Sage.

Larned, Emily. 2016. 'Publishing as (Socially Engaged) Practice.' *Book Art Theory* (blog). September 15, 2016, https://www.collegebookart.org/bookarttheory/4247519.

Latour, Bruno. 1999. *Pandora's Hope: Essays on the Reality of Science Studies*. Cambridge: Harvard University Press.

LensCulture. 2017. 'The Best and Worst of Times: Talking Photobooks With Aperture's Lesley Martin.' Accessed February 22, 2021. https://www.lensculture.com/articles/aperture-foundation-the-best-and-worst-of-times-talking-photobooks-with-aperture-s-lesley-martin.

Levine, Gemma. 1987. *Gemma Levine's Faces of the 80s*. London: Collins.

Lippard, Lucy. 1985. 'Conspicuous Consumption: New Artists' Books'. In *Artists' Books: A Critical Anthology and Sourcebook*, edited by Joan Lyons, 49–58. Rochester: Visual Studies Workshop Press.

Long, Jonathan. 2016. 'Photobooks in the Real World: Look! Modernity.' *Source Photographic Review*, winter 2016, issue 88.

Lubben, Kristen. 2019. 'Partial Histories.' In *How We See: Photobooks by Women*, by Russet Lederman, Olga Yatskevich, and Michael Lang, 13–17. New York: 10x10 Photobooks.

Ludovico, Alessandro. 2013. *Post-Digital Print: The Mutation of Publishing since 1894*. Eindhoven: Onomatopee.

Lyons, Joan, ed. 1985. *Artists' Books : A Critical Anthology and Sourcebook*. Rochester: Visual Studies Workshop Press.

Maclean, Rachel. 2016. *Again and Again and Again*. Video, 03:14. https://artcollection.salford.ac.uk/rachel-maclean-again-and-again-and-again/.

Mahmoodian, Amak. 2016. *Shenasnameh*. Bristol: RRB Photobooks and ICVL.

———. 2019. *Zanjir*. Bristol: RRB Photobooks and ICVL.

Marcopoulos, Ari, and Mahfuz Sultan. 2019. *Ari Marcopoulos: Entropy*. Amsterdam: Roma.

Martin, Lesley. 2014. 'Publisher's Note in The Photobook Review.' *The Photobook Review*, fall 2014, volume 7.

———. 2017. 'Invitation to a Taxonomy of the Contemporary Photobook.' In *Photobook Phenomenon*, edited by CCCB, Moritz Neumüller, and Fundació Foto Colectania, 11–14. Barcelona: RM.

———. 2018. 'The Offset Artist.' January 5, 2018, https://aperture.org/editorial/pbr-singh/.

Miles, Melissa. 2010. 'The Drive to Archive: Conceptual Documentary Photobook Design.' *Photographies* 3 no.1: 49–68. https://doi.org/10.1080/17540760903561108.

Minsky, Richard. 2016. 'College Book Art Association – Book Art Theory Blog Mission Statement.' *Book Art Theory* (blog). October 15, 2016, https://collegebookart.org/bookarttheory/4302822/Reply?replyTo=9266226#9266226.

Miss Read. 2018. *Publishing Manifestos*. Berlin: Miss Read.

Monzón, Óscar. 2013. *Karma*. Paris: RVB Books.

Moreiras, Camila. 2017. 'Joan Fontcuberta: Post-Photography and the Spectral Image of Saturation.' *Journal of Spanish Cultural Studies* 18 no.1: 57–77. https://doi.org/10.1080/14636204.2016.1274496.

Morel, Aron. 2020. 'Field Exchange with Tommaaso Parillo & Arom Morel.' *YET*, 2020, issue 12.

Morris, Lindsay. 2015a. 'Resources – Children's Books'. Accessed May 15, 2020, https://www.youareyouproject.com/childrens-books.

———. 2015b. *You Are You*. Heidelberg: Kehrer Heidelberg.

Nan, Lu. 2018. *Trilogy*. London: GOST books.

Neumüller, Moritz. 2017. 'By the Book.' In *Photobook Phenomenon*, edited by CCCB, Moritz Neumüller, and Fundació Foto Colectania, 3–7. Barcelona: RM.

Neves, José Luís Afonso. 2017. 'The Many Faces of the Photobook: Establishing the Origins of Photobookwork Practice.' PhD diss., Ulster University.

Noble, Andrea. 2016. 'Photobooks in the Real World: Violence in Colombia.' *Source Photographic Review*, winter 2016, issue 88.

Offset Projects. 2020. 'guftgu with Susanna Chung.' Filmed October 21, 2020. Video 1:11:24. https://www.youtube.com/watch?v=sjDo10JydAo&t=3838s.

O'Hagan, Sean. 2015. 'Hidden Islam – 479 Comments: The Photobook That Contains No Photos.' *The Guardian*, January 12, 2015, http://www.theguardian.com/artanddesign/ 2015/jan/09/hidden-islam-479-comments-nicolo-degiorgis-sean-o-hagan.

Olthof, Eva. 2015. *Return to Rightful Owner*. Eindhoven: Onomatopee.

On Demand Books. 2016. 'Espresso Book Machine.' Accessed July 5, 2018, http://www.ondemandbooks.com/.

Openshaw, Jonathan. 2015. *Postdigital Artisans: Craftmanship with a New Aesthetic in Fashion, Art, Design and Architecture*. Amsterdam: Frame Publishers BV.

Oursler, Stephanie. 1976. *Un Album Di Violenza*. Rome: Edizione delle donne.

Oyarzabal, Gloria. 2020. *Woman Go No'Gree*. Barcelona: Editorial RM

Palu, Louie. 2019. *A Field Guide to Asbestos*. n.p.: Yoffy Press.

Pantall, Colin. 2012. 'Introspective, Navel-Gazing Nitpickers.' *Colin Pantall's Blog* (blog). January 10, 2012, http://colinpantall.blogspot.co.uk/2012/01/introspective-navel-gazing-nitpickers.html.

Paradox. 2016. 'Projects Archive.' Accessed September 2, 2019, http://www.paradox.nl/project/platforms/education.

Parr, Martin, and Wassink Lundgren. 2015. *The Chinese Photobook: From the 1900s to the Present*. New York: Aperture.

Parr, Martin, Lesley Martin, Ramon Reverté, Marcelo Brodsky and Lata Cannabrava. 2011. 'A Note from the

Advisory Committee.' In *The Latin American Photobook*, edited by Horacio Fernández, 7. New York: Aperture.

Paul, Christiane. 2015. 'From Immateriality to Neomateriality: Art and the Conditions of Digital Materiality'. Paper presented at International Symposium on Electronic Art, Vancouver, 2015. New York: International Symposium on Electronic Art International, http://www.isea-archives.org/docs/2015/proceedings/ISEA2015_proceedings.pdf.

Pearce, Nathan. 2014. *Midwest Dirt*. Fairfield: Same Coin Press.

———. 2015. *Midwest Dirt*. Bootleg ed. Fairfield: Same Coin Press.

Philipsen, Lotte. 2014. 'Who's Afraid of the Audience? – Digital and Post-Digital Perspectives on Aesthetics.' *A Peer Reviewed Journal About*. 3 no.1 http://www.aprja.net/whos-afraid-of-the-audience-digital-and-post-digital-perspectives-on-aesthetics/.

Phillpot, Clive. 2013. *Booktrek. Selected Essays on Artists' Books since 1972*. Zurich: JRP Ringier.

Photobook Museum. 2015. *The PhotoBookMuseum*. Cologne: The PhotoBookMuseum.

PhotoBooks. 2019. 'About.' Facebook. Accessed November 11, 2019, https://www.facebook.com/groups/photobookgroup/.

Pink, Sarah, Heather A. Horst, John Postill, Larissa Hjorth, Tania Lewis and Jo Tacchi, eds. 2016. *Digital Ethnography: Principles and Practice*. Los Angeles: SAGE.

Pongo, Léonard. 2013. *A Certain Kind of Energy*. Brussels: Léonard Pongo.

Printed Matter. 2021a. 'The Classroom – Thursday, February 25.' Filmed February 25, 2021. Video, 9:59:15. https://www.youtube.com/watch?v=YceuODFENoE.

———. 2021b. 'Contemporary Artists' Books Conference – Friday, February 26.' Filmed February 26, 2021. Video, 3:28:12. https://www.youtube.com/watch?v=ZSD7Ku-H19AY&t=3057s.

———. 2021c. 'Contemporary Artists' Books Conference – Saturday, February 27.' Filmed February 27, 2021. Video, 8:25:06. https://www.youtube.com/watch?v=7LaSsDZPkN8&t=8s.

Rafal, Ethan. 2015. *Shock and Awe*. SanFrancisco: IHA Editions

Rasti, Laurence. 2017. *There Are No Homosexuals in Iran*. Zurich: Edition Patrick Frey.

Related Tactics. 2019. *Shelf Life*. San Francisco: Related Tactics.

Rheingold, Howard. 1993. *The Virtual Community: Homesteading on the Electronic Frontier*. Reading: Addison-Wesley.

Rio Branco, Miguel. 1998. *Silent book*. São Paulo: Cosac & Naify.

Rivetti, Ermanno. 2012. 'Artists' Books: The Marriage of Text and Image.' In *Art:Book*, edited by Bim Hjortrontseen et al., 16–18. London: London College of Communication.

Rochat, Maya. 2018. *A Rock Is a River*. London: SPBH Editions.

Rohdie, Sam. 2006. *Montage*. Cinema Aesthetics. Manchester: Manchester University Press.

Rose, Amelie, and Daria Tuminas. 2020. 'Is a Book Worth a Tree?' *YET*, 2020, issue 12.

Roth, Andrew. 2001. *The Book of 101 Books: Seminal Photographic Books of the Twentieth Century*. New York: PPP Editions.

Roth, Andrew and The Hasselblad Center. 2004. *The Open Book: A History of the Photographic Book from 1878 to the Present*. Vol. 1. Gothenburg: Hasselblad Center.

Rubinstein, Daniel, and Katrina Sluis. 2013. 'The Digital Image in Photographic Culture: Algorithmic Photography and the Crisis of Representation.' In *The Photographic Image in Digital Culture*, edited by Martin Lister, 2nd ed., 22–40. London: Taylor & Francis.

Rule, Dan. 2015. 'Editor's Note.' *Photofile*, spring/summer 2015, volume 97.

RVB Books. 2016. 'RVB Books - Karma by Óscar Monzón.' Accessed July 26, 2017, https://rvb-books.com/book.php?id_book=54.

Samolet, Igor. 2013. *Be Happy!* Berlin: Peperoni books.

Schaden, M. 2013. 'Here Comes the Digital Photobook!' *European Photography*, 2013, issue 93.

Schellekens, Viory. 2019. 'Photobooks of 2019, the List Makers.' Facebook. December 4, 2019, https://www.facebook.com/Viory.Schellekens/posts/photobooks-of-2019here-is-the-meta-listits-february-6-2020-when-i-conclude-the-m/2509730949095893/.

Schles, Ken. 1988. *Invisible City*. Pasadena: Twelvetrees Press.

Self Publish, Be Happy. 2018. 'Photobook RESET Hosted by C/O Berlin.' Accessed March 3, 2019, http://selfpublishbehappy.com/2018/12/photobook-reset-hosted-by-co-berlin/.

Shannon, Elizabeth. 2010. 'The Rise of the Photobook in the Twenty- First Century.' *St Andrews Journal of Art History and Museum Studies* 14: 55–62.

Shaw, Tate. 2016. *Blurred Library: Essays on Artists' Books*. Victoria: Cuneiform.

Shisui, Tanahashi. 1974. *Ryurai Ryukyo 1954–1973*. Tanahashi Shisui.

Simon, Joshua. 2012. *Neomaterialism*. Berlin: Sternberg Press.

Singh, Dyanita. 1986. *Zakir Hussain*. Singapore: Himalayan Books.

———. 2005. *Chairs*. Göttingen: Steidl and the Isabella Stewart Gardner Museum.

Smyth, D., Bruno Ceschel, Aron Morel, Hannah Watson, Maxwell Anderson, and Damian Poulain. 2015. 'London Calling.' *The British Journal of Photography*, June 2015, volume 162, issue 7836.

Solo, David, and F Chiocchetti. 2020. 'In the Mood for Books, David Solo in Conversation with Frederica Chiocchetti.' *YET*, 2020, issue 12.

Spowart, Doug. 2015a. 'PHOTOBOOKS: Everyone a Publisher.' *La Trobe Journal* 95: 105–14.

———. 2015b.'Photobook Anxiety – A Paper by Doug Spowart.' *Wotwedid* (blog). September 3, 2015, https://wotwedid.com/2015/09/03/photobook-anxiety-a-paper-by-doug-spowart/.

———. 2018. 'A Spectrum: Photobook to Artist's Book.' *Wot We Did* (blog). January, 2015, https://wotwedid. com/2018/04/13/a-photo-spectrum-photobook-to-artists-book/.

———. 2019. 'Antipodean Photobook Tribes – Keynote Talk'. *Antipodean Photobook*. Novemebr 14, 2019, https://theantipodeanphotobook.com/ 2019/11/14/antipodean-photobook- tribes-keynote-talk-bifb-photobook-weekend/.

Stadler, Matthew. 2018.'The Ends of the Book: Reading, Economies and Publics.' In *Publishing Manifestos*, edited by Michalis Pichler, 118–27. Miss Read.

Steyerl, Hito. 2012. *The Wretched of the Screen; E-flux Journal* 6. Berlin: Sternberg Press.

Sully, Isabelle, Elaine W Ho, Beatrix Pang, and Yin Yin Wong. 2019. *Publication Studio Portable: A Mobile Publishing Manual*. Hong Kong: Publication Studio Pearl River Delta.

Sweetman, Alex. 1985. 'Photobookworks: The Critical Realist Tradition.' In *Artists' Books: A Critical Anthology and Sourcebook*, edited by Joan Lyons, 187–207. Rochester: Visual Studies Workshop Press.

Taffel, Sy. 2015. 'Perspectives on the Postdigital.' *Convergence* 22 no.3: 324–38. https://doi.org/10.1177/1354856514567827.

Tagg, John. 1988. *The Burden of Representation: Essays on Photographies and Histories*. New York: Macmillan Education.

Tannenbaum, Barbara. 2012. *DIY: Photographers & Books*. Cleveland: Cleveland Museum of Art.

Tate. 2012. 'Daido Moriyama Printing Show.' Accessed October 10, 2017, http://www.tate.org.uk/whats-on/tate-modern/performance/daido-moriyama-printing-show.

———. n.d. 'Photobook – Art Term.' Accessed February 21, 2017, https://www.tate.org.uk/art/art-terms/p/photobook.

Temporary Services. 2014. *Publishing in the Realm of Plant Fibres and Electrons*. Chicago: Temporary Services.

The Photobook Museum, and Montag Stiftung Kunst und Gesellschaft. 2020. *The Photobook in Art and Society: Participative Potentials of a Medium*. Berlin; Cologne: Jovis ; The PhotoBook Museum.

The PhotoBookMuseum. 2014. *The PhotoBookMuseum*. Cologne: The PhotoBookMuseum.

Thoburn, Nicholas. 2016. Anti-Book: *On the Art and Politics of Radical Publishing*. Minneapolis: University of Minnesota Press.

Tuminas, Daria, and Moritz Neumüller. 2017. *Market? What Market?*. Amsterdam: Photobook Week Aarhus and Unseen. https://www.docdroid.net/VBrMMun/market-what-market-booklet-pdf.

Vanthuyne, Stefan, and Moritz Neumüller. 2017. 'Belgian Platform For Photobook'. *Belphotobooks* (blog).

November 3, 2017, http://belphotobooks.org/photobook-phenomenon/.

Vartanian, Ivan. 2009. 'The Japanese Photobook Toward an Immediate Medium'. In *Japanese Photobooks of the 1960s and '70s*, by Ryūichi Kaneko and Ivan Vartanian, 11–23. New York: Aperture.

Verity, Adam. 2012. 'Print/Screen: Current and Future Dissemination of the Self-Published Artist's Book.'. In *Photography and the Artist's Book*, edited by Theresa Wilkie, Jonathan Carson, and Rosie Miller, 90–107. Edinburgh: MuseumsEtc.

Vestberg, Nina. 2016. 'There Is No Cloud: Toward a Materialist Ecology of Post-Photography.' *Captures* 1 no.1. http://revuecaptures.org/node/448.

Vitale, Salvatore. 2020. 'Other Worlds in the Weekend Paper.' *YET*, 2020, issue 12.

Vitale, Salvatore, Nicolas Polli, and Elena Vaninetti. 2020. 'Editor's Note.' *YET*, 2020, issue 12.

Wainwright, Jean. 2015. *Border Line: Rights of Passage.* Performance and publication, May 6-8, 2015, Venice Agendas, Venice.

Walker, Ian. 2012. 'A Kind of a 'Huh?': The Siting of Twentysix Gasoline Stations (1962).' In *The Photobook, From Talbot to Ruscha and Beyond*, edited by Patrizia Di Bello, Colette Wilson and Shamoon Zamir, 111–28. London: I.B Tauris.

Webb, Sheila. 2013. 'Art Commentary for the Middlebrow: Promoting Modernism & Modern Art through Popular Culture – How Life Magazine Brought 'The New' into Middle-Class Homes.' *American Journalism* 27 no.3: 115–50.

Weijde, Eric van der. 2018. '4478ZINE Publishing Manifesto.' In *Publishing Manifestos*, edited by Michalis Pichler, 144–45. Miss Read.

Weijde, Erik van der. 2017. *This Is Not My Book*. Leipzig: Spector Books.

Wilkie, Theresa, Jonathan Carson, and Rosie Miller, eds. 2012. *Photography and theArtist's Book.* Edinburgh: MuseumsEtc.

Wilkie, Theresa, and Jane Pendlebury. 2012. 'Locating Photography and the Artist's Book.' In *Photography and the Artist's Book*, edited by Theresa Wilkie, Jonathan Carson, and Rosie Miller, 62–89. Edinburgh: MuseumsEtc.

Willett, Amani. 2017. *The Disappearance of Joseph Plummer.* London: Overlapse.

———. 2020. *A Parallel Road.* London: Overlapse.

Wirth, Karen. 1995. 'Re-Reading the Boundless Book.' In *Talking the Boundless Book: Art, Language, and the Book Arts: Essays from Art & Language, Re-Reading the Boundless Book*, edited by Dick Higgins and Charles Alexander, 137–44. Minneapolis: Minnesota Center for Book Arts.

Wolukau-Wanambwa, Stanley. 2019. 'The paradoxically perfect and utterly imperfect photobook.' *Belphotobooks* (blog). August 15, 2019, https://belphotobooks.org/the-paradoxically-perfect-and-utterly-imperfect-photobook/.

Yenelouis, Bernard. 2013. 'No Center, No Periphery.' In *10x10 American Photobooks*, edited by Russet Lederman, Olga Yatskevich, and Matthew Carson, 14–15. New York: 10x10 Photobooks.

Yukichi, Watabe. 2011. *Watabe Yukichi: A Criminal Investigation*. Paris: Barral.

Zimmermann, Philip. 2016. 'Photobook to Photobook-work, a Spectrum'. *College Book Art Association* (blog). July 1, 2016, https://www.collegebookart.org/bookarttheory/4109494.

Matt Johnston is a visual practitioner, researcher and educator in the UK currently working as an Assistant Professor at Coventry University where he leads the MA Photography programme. For the past decade his work has concentrated on the photobook and its accompanying ecology, instigating a global reading initiative called The Photobook Club in 2010 and seeking to bring new audiences to the medium with projects and publications like *Invisible City: A Digital* Resource (2012), the Box of Books (2013-15) and *The Make and Look Lockdown Book* (2020). Matt has spoken and written about the photobook in a variety of spaces including the London Design Festival, ELISIVA school of design, Arts Libris, The Photobook Review and *Code-X: Paper, Ink, Pixel and Screen.* He completed his PhD at the University for the Creative Arts in 2020. (mjohnstonphotography.co.uk)

Emmanuelle Waeckerlé is a Reader in fine art and relational practices at UCA Farnham and director of bookRoom since 2009. Her research and practice have evolved from the single discipline of fine art photography into multiple, interconnected work zones: conceptual writing, performance, new musical composition and artist-publishing. Recent publications include *A Direction out There, Readwalking (with) Thoreau* (2021), *Ode (owed) to O* (2017), *Reading (story of) O* (2015), *RISE WITH YOUR CLASS NOT FROM IT* (2016) and *Code X - Paper, Pixel, Ink and Screen* (2015). Some of her artist publications are held in collections including the V&A, the Poetry Library at Southbank Centre, UWE, The Bibliotheque Nationale de France and the Centre Des Livres d'Artistes. (ewaeckerle.com)

Author
Matt Johnston

Editor
Emmanuelle Waeckerlé

Graphic design
Studio Ward Goes
Assistant: Juul van der Zandt

Text editor
Melissa Larner

Image editors
Matt Johnston and Ward Goes

Advisor
Freek Lomme

Printer
Printon AS

Typefaces
GT Pressura Regular, GT America Regular
and GT America Italic (Grilli Type)

ONOMATOPEE 220

Photobooks &
a critical companion to the
contemporary medium
By Matt Johnston

ISBN: 978-94-93148-65-9

Made possible thanks to the generous support of the University for the Creative Arts.

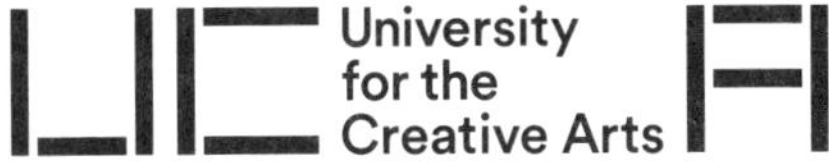

Special thanks to Terry Perk and bookRoom research platform at the University for the Creative Arts.

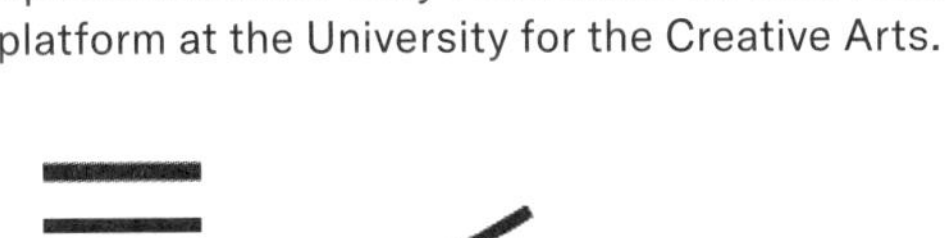

First edition, 2021

Onomatopee Projects
www.onomatopee.net

Acknowledgements — I am thankful to many people who have helped form the research on which this book is built, and aided its life on these pages. My thanks to Emmanuelle Waeckerlé for continuing the critical conversations we started seven years ago and helping to shape and sharpen this publication, to Terry Perk and the University for the Creative Arts for their generous support in making Photobooks & possible, to Ward Goes and Juul van der Zandt for constructing a book that embodies my emphasis on conversation between maker and reader, and to Freek Lomme and Onomatopee for seeing the merit and place of this conversation in a respected catalogue. For their assistance in my original PhD research or critical eye as this book developed, I would also like to thank Jean Wainwright, Camille Baker, Juan Cires, Kelly Bryan, Anthony Luvera, Emma Lambert, Dan Bosworth, Doug Spowart, Victoria Cooper, Rich Higginbottom, Melissa Larner and all those who gave time and thought to the interviews and surveys featured in these pages. Finally, my thanks go to the community of global readers that are The Photobook Club and who have provided a constant source of inspiration for my research.